DIS/CONSENT

DIS/CONSENT

Perspectives on Sexual Consent
and Sexual Violence

edited by KelleyAnne Malinen

FERNWOOD PUBLISHING
HALIFAX & WINNIPEG

Editing: Erin Seatter
Cover design: Tania Craan
Printed and bound in Canada

Published by Fernwood Publishing
32 Oceanvista Lane, Black Point, Nova Scotia, B0J 1B0
and 748 Broadway Avenue, Winnipeg, Manitoba, R3G 0X3
www.fernwoodpublishing.ca

Judge Lenehan's decision is reprinted with permission from CBC.

Fernwood Publishing Company Limited gratefully acknowledges the financial support of the Government of Canada, the Canada Council for the Arts, the Manitoba Department of Culture, Heritage and Tourism under the Manitoba Publishers Marketing Assistance Program and the Province of Manitoba, through the Book Publishing Tax Credit, for our publishing program. We are pleased to work in partnership with the Province of Nova Scotia to develop and promote our creative industries for the benefit of all Nova Scotians.

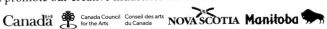

Library and Archives Canada Cataloguing in Publication

Title: Dis/consent: perspectives on sexual consent and
sexual violence / edited by KelleyAnne Malinen.
Names: Malinen, KelleyAnne, 1979– editor.
Description: Includes bibliographical references and index.
Identifiers: Canadiana (print) 20190065753 | Canadiana
(ebook) 20190065893 | ISBN 9781773630892 (softcover) | ISBN
9781773630908 (EPUB) | ISBN 9781773630915 (Kindle)
Subjects: LCSH: Sex crimes—Canada. | LCSH: Sexual
consent—Canada. | LCSH: Rape—Canada.
Classification: LCC HV6593.C3 D57 2019 | DDC 364.15/320971—dc23

CONTENTS

CONTRIBUTORS

ANNELIES COOPER

Annelies Cooper is a PhD candidate in political science at York University. Her research inquires into the logics and technologies of settler-colonial governance through the implementation of Canada's legal duty to consult and accommodate Indigenous Peoples. She is a founding member of Silence is Violence at York University.

MAYA EICHLER

Maya Eichler is Canada Research Chair in Social Innovation and Community Engagement and assistant professor in the Department of Political and Canadian Studies and the Department of Women's Studies at Mount Saint Vincent University. Her research interests lie in the transition from military to civilian life, gender and the armed forces, military families, and the privatization of military security. From 2015 to 2017, she co-chaired the 5th Canadian Division and Mount Saint Vincent University Operation Honour Community Working Group.

CHANELLE GALLANT

Chanelle Gallant is a long-time organizer, trainer, and writer with a focus on sex and justice. Her writing has appeared in MTV News, TruthOut, the Rumpus, *Bitch* magazine, and various anthologies. For over a decade, she has organized to build the power of people in the sex trade and to end policing and prisons. In 2016, she helped found the first chapter of

Showing Up for Racial Justice outside of the United States. She is working on her first book, a theory of sexual labour.

MANDI GRAY

Mandi Gray is a PhD candidate in sociology at York University. She recently completed a feature-length documentary film titled *Slut or Nut: The Diary of a Rape Trial* <www.slutornut.ca)>, which premiered at Hot Docs in May 2018. Mandi's work blends creativity, activism, and sociology in order to prevent and respond to sexual violence. She co-founded Silence is Violence at York University in 2015, inspired by her own experience of reporting sexual assault on campus in the first year of her doctoral studies.

EL JONES

El Jones is a poet, educator, journalist, and advocate. She was the fifth poet laureate of Halifax and currently holds the 15th Nancy's Chair in Women's Studies at Mount Saint Vincent University. El is a co-founder of the *Black Power Hour,* a radio show developed collectively with prisoners. Her advocacy and work fight anti-Black racism in Canada, walking in the path of our great-grandmothers, who resisted relentlessly.

KELLEYANNE MALINEN

KelleyAnne Malinen is an assistant professor in the Sociology and Anthropology Department at Mount Saint Vincent University. She does research in the area of sexual violence and has published several journal articles about sexual violence committed by women, against women. She also studies racist ideology masquerading as free speech advocacy, and racism in the education system. KelleyAnne strives for intersectionality in her teaching.

MSVU FEMINIST COLLECTIVE

The MSVU Feminist Collective is a student initiative dedicated to promoting gender equity and advocating against sexist attitudes and actions, on campus and in our communities. The collective seeks to engage with feminist issues as they are relevant to our lives as students and otherwise.

The collective also aims to be a platform for discussion, education, and activism, and strives to uphold an intersectional feminist perspective.

SAN PATTEN

San Patten has an MSc in community health sciences from the University of Calgary. Her consulting practice (San Patten and Associates) has operated since 2005 in Canada and globally, grounded in principles of human rights and the social determinants of health, and specializing in HIV prevention, community-based research, policy analysis, and program evaluation. San also provides facilitation, strategic planning, scenario planning, and conflict mediation services. She is a university educator in social policy, the non-profit sector, sustainability, and health promotion.

DEBRA PARIS PERRY

Debra Paris Perry wants to live in a world where people involved in the sex trade are afforded the same respect, compassion, and understanding as any other human being. As a woman who has been in and around the sex trade for more than forty years, she has been applauded by many for her informative and sometimes raw presentations on this topic. When she's not working as the outreach coordinator for the Uniacke Centre for Community Development, a program of In My Own Voice (iMove) Arts Association, or working for the YWCA, she can be found talking to people on the street, trying to help with whatever they need. Debra is in the process of writing an autobiography.

SHERRY PICTOU

Sherry Pictou is a Mi'kmaw woman from L'sitkuk (water cuts through high rocks), known as Bear River First Nation, Nova Scotia, and an assistant professor with a focus on Indigenous feminism in the Women's Studies Department at Mount Saint Vincent University. She is also a former chief for her community and the former co-chair of the World Forum of Fisher Peoples. Her research interests are decolonization of treaty relations, social justice for Indigenous women, Indigenous women's role in food and lifeways, and Indigenous knowledge and food systems.

LAURA PIN

Laura Pin is a PhD candidate in political science at York University. Her research investigates the politics of participation, specifically the relationship between participatory democracy and neoliberal restructuring in cities. She is a founding member of Silence is Violence, an experientially led collective that aims to address institutional forms of sexual violence on university campuses.

MEREDITH RALSTON

Meredith Ralston is a professor in the Department of Women's Studies and Department of Political Studies at Mount Saint Vincent University and an award-winning documentary filmmaker. She has directed six documentaries (two with the National Film Board of Canada) on women and politics, women's organizing, sex work, and sex tourism. She has written or co-written two books, with a third book, *Slut-Shaming and Whore-Phobia: The Unfinished Sexual Revolution,* to be published in 2019. Her research interests are in the areas of prostitution and sex trafficking, and women's involvement in politics.

ALAN SANTINELE MARTINO

Alan Santinele Martino is a PhD candidate in sociology at McMaster University. He has received prestigious research awards, including the Ontario Trillium Award. His primary areas of interest include the sociology of sexualities, sociology of gender, and critical disability studies, as well as their intersections. His main body of work investigates the romantic and sexual experiences of adults with intellectual disabilities in Ontario, by putting into conversation theories from the sociology of sexualities and critical disability studies.

ALISON SYMINGTON

Alison Symington holds a law degree from the University of Toronto and a master's degree in international legal studies from New York University. Previously, she was the co-director of research and advocacy at the Canadian HIV/AIDS Legal Network. In this role she pioneered feminist analysis of the criminalization of HIV non-disclosure, including producing two documentaries. She has also worked with LEAF (Women's Legal Education and Action Fund) on issues of sexual assault and HIV criminalization.

ARDATH WHYNACHT

Ardath Whynacht is an activist and professor who lives on unceded Mi'kmaw territory. She teaches sociology at Mount Allison University and in the federal prison system. She is currently running a SSHRC-funded research project on violence, kinship, and transformative justice and working on a book about emotional labour and transformative practice.

ANDREA ZANIN

Andrea Zanin is a queer writer, scholar, teacher, community organizer, and expert witness who focuses on the ethics of BDSM/leather and non-monogamy. She has been published in the *Globe and Mail, Bitch* and *Ms.* magazines, and many anthologies, both popular and scholarly. Andrea was named Toronto Leather Pride Woman of the Year 2014 and won the Pantheon of Leather Canadian Award for 2016. She is currently working on a book and plans to soon return to finish her PhD in gender, feminist, and women's studies at York University. Read her at <www.sexgeek.wordpress.com> or find her on Twitter at @sexgeekAZ.

ACKNOWLEDGEMENTS

I would like first to acknowledge the thoughtfulness and commitment of contributors to this volume. All of you have been wonderful to work with. El Jones, Ardath Whynacht, and Sherry Pictou, you helped me to think through the expected and unexpected complexities of this work. Thanks to San Patten for suggesting the title *Dis/Consent.*

There are folks I would like to thank for helping me get to this great spot in my life and career where book editing is possible. First, of course, are my parents, who have provided constant support, lots of great conversation, and a good deal of childcare as well. Others are friends (one or two of whom I have lost touch with) —Tina Roberts-Jeffers, Thomas Henderson, Andrea Smith, Pierre Loiselle, Julie Moffet, François Quirion-Blais, Nancy Mallet, and Amanda Crocker.

I also thank the Sociology and Anthropology Department at Mount Saint Vincent University for providing me a space in the world to work from.

Finally, thanks to my acquisition and development editor, Candida Hadley, who has been a wonderful resource and advisor; to the two anonymous reviewers, whose comments have been so constructive; and to Erin Seatter, for the careful and insightful copy editing.

Chapter 1

DIS/CONSENT

An Introduction

KelleyAnne Malinen

This volume contains thirteen chapters of disconsent directed to social structures and institutions that produce or enable sexual violence, and that disallow or delegitimize sexual consent. The insights generated in this text resonate with the work of queer disabilities scholar Abby Wilkerson, which inspired *Dis/Consent* before its contributors were assembled. Wilkerson (2002) identifies consistent patterns in relationships between sexual autonomy and social power. Those with more power in society are granted greater opportunity to give or withhold consent and to be safe both from sexual violence and sexual stigmatization. Those with less power are more likely to find the consent they give negated or stigmatized and are more likely to be subjected to sexual violence. Thus, "oppressed groups generally tend to *share* the experience of being particularly subject to ero-tophobic judgements of their sexual behaviors or 'natures', [in addition to] restrictions against practices associated with them, [and] sexual violence and harassment" (41). Following Wilkerson, *Dis/Consent* is inspired by recognition of "sexual harms as a significant force in perpetuating the inequality of *any* oppressed group" (35). As such, *Dis/Content* brings variously positioned voices to conversations about sexual violence and sexual consent.

WHAT IS "DIS/CONSENT"?

The concept of dis/consent was selected as a title (following the suggestion of contributor San Patten) for its capacity to hold a multitude of characteristics and broad themes that animate the coming chapters:

- "Dis/consent" bears a strong resemblance to "discontent," which indicates an individual's or group's dissatisfaction with their circumstances or treatment. Social movements are widely understood to emerge from discontent.
- "Dis/consent" contains "dissent." The texts brought together here express dissent against the overlapping power structures that sustain a status quo under which sexual autonomy of marginalized groups is negated.
- "Dis/consent" contains "consent." Consent as the basis for all human sexuality is an organizing aspiration of this volume. Very simply, sexual activity should be undertaken only under conditions of enthusiastic consent from those involved.
- The prefix "dis" indicates a reversal or a contrary force. "Dis/consent" can also be read as a critique of the notion of consent as it is commonly presented in popular culture. Too often, consent is understood as a kind of currency, typically passed from women to men, in decontextualized exchanges. In reality, moments of consent or non-consent always occur in a social context, where power is at play. The institutional and structural themes introduced here draw into question simplistic and individualistic understandings of consent.
- By attending to the "dis" in another way, we can read "dis/consent" as a term referring to sexual violence, which is what is left when consent is not present in a sexual interaction. Sexual violence is one of the central problematics taken up by this volume.

THE STRUCTURE OF *DIS/CONSENT*

Heterogenous Texture

The chapters found here are written in a range of styles, including formally academic, dialogic, journalistic, and first-person voice. By creating a heterogeneous conversation, *Dis/Consent* provides a window on the multiplex perspectives and stakes at play in matters of sexual violence and sexual consent. It is hoped that most readers who engage with this volume will find themselves outside the familiar at one moment or another, whether by meeting with a perspective produced outside the academy or inside the academy, or by meeting unfamiliar cultural terminology or a never-before-considered set of concerns.

The heterogeneity of this volume is not only about style but also about points of view. While all of the perspectives that appear in this volume are animated by some pursuit of a less violent society, the authors sometimes have quite different, even conflicting, ideas about what needs to change and how. For example, while both contributors favour decriminalizing sex work, Ralston emphasizes the sexual autonomy sex workers have, whereas Paris Perry emphasizes the structural and intergenerational factors that can push women into sex work and the violence women can encounter there. Such diversity of perspectives provides readers with intellectual space and fodder for exploring the complexities that inform research and activism against sexual violence.

Norman Fairclough (2003) lists a number of possible orientations that texts may display toward difference. With its range of voices and perspectives, *Dis/Consent* intends to practise the orientation Fairclough describes as "an openness to, acceptance of, recognition of difference; an exploration of difference, as in 'dialogue' in the richest sense of the term" (41). This orientation toward difference suits a project interested in sexual consent insofar as sexual violence is a failure to recognize or accept that the other person need neither share nor submit to the perpetrator's desires. Put simply, when one person accepts that a second person doesn't have to want or do what the first person wants, the first person will not sexually assault the second person. In this sense, openness to difference can be understood as the antithesis of violence.

Cyclic Structure

Dis/Consent begins and ends — or is wrapped by — the work of Indigenous scholar Sherry Pictou, who writes from a Mi'kmaw woman's perspective. Between Pictou's chapters appear two sections containing five chapters each, further described below. On one level, this wrapping serves a chronological function. The opening chapter, "Beginnings and Renewal,

Oppression and Fragmentation," recalls a time when Mi'kmaw women and girls had yet to be confronted with the gendered and colonial ideologies that undergird so many rape myths and that lead disproportionately to violence against Indigenous women and girls. It then describes ongoing histories of settler-colonial oppression that have been profoundly interconnected with sexualized violence against Indigenous women. The closing chapter, "Survival and Resurgence," ends the volume by addressing the theme of Indigenous women's ongoing survival of colonialism and offers ways to address interlinked aspects of oppression in collaboration with allies.

The overlay between "Beginnings and Renewal" and "Survival and Resurgence" draws this text into a circuit and thereby supports non-linear thinking. A recent article by performance studies scholar Rebecca Schneider (2018), "That the Past May Yet Have Another Future: Gesture in the Times of Hands Up," helps to relay the power of this circuit. Schneider's paper underlines the presence of history in any current moment. It situates within settler-colonial horizons gendered and racialized forms of violence, to which we could add violence in homophobic/heterosexist, cisnormative, and ableist forms. We are, Schneider argues, in relationships with and indebted to people of the past, present, and future. This volume exemplifies such relationships, including relationships of indebtedness: Chapters of *Dis/Consent* have been written, many by white settlers, in the unceded ancestral homelands of the Mi'kmaq, Anishinabeg, Haudenosaunee, Wendat, and Métis Nations. They were also written in territories built for white people through both the labour of enslaved Black people and the exclusion of Black people from institutions that distribute power.

In this era when the earth is imperilled under conditions of capitalist exploitation and extraction, within a system that distributes both precarity and time unevenly, Schneider views non-linear thinking, such as the circular structure proposed here, as essential to positive social change. She cites Damien Sojoyner (2017: 296): "The trick and the abject horror of time is its covert use in the reinforcement of difference (i.e., race, gender, sexuality)." Sojoyner's original text argues that time is applied "harshly" to Black people, for example, through "time served" in prisons. On the other hand, time is treated as "unbounded" and envisioned in terms of "development and progress," manipulated in the service of expansion, exploitation and extraction when applied to white people, who "habitually re-create [themselves] as subjects and inheritors of the privileges of the colonial-capital nation state" (300).

Time also covertly reinforces difference through dominant understandings of sexual violence and sexual consent. Feminists and anti-rape activists have long fought to make it understood that consent to sexual activity in one moment does not last a lifetime. Survivors of sexual violence of all genders are also socially stigmatized. The stigma — an oppressive construct from the start — long outlasts the experiences it is initially attached to. What would it mean to have a culture accountable to histories of sexual violence? What would it mean to create sexually non-violent futures for coming generations?

Schneider cites Sisseton-Wahpeton Oyate scholar-scientist Kim TallBear in arguing for research that works "*in less linear ways*" and researchers who "stand with" communities and are "willing to be altered" through the research relationship (305). The collection of chapters within *Dis/Consent* aspires to represent a standing together across communities. With this direction in mind, the final word of the final chapter was written by Pictou, who speaks of resurgence from a Mi'kmaw woman's perspective.

Legislation, Policy, and Government

The first of the two sections that appear between the opening and closing chapters of *Dis/Consent*, entitled "Legislation, Policy, and Government," contains chapters that address colonial institutions as they relate to matters of sexual violence and consent. These chapters detail various aspects of the workings of these institutions. Three focus on the structure or operation of Canadian law: "The Bogus BDSM Defence: The Manipulation of Kink as Consent to Assault" (Gallant and Zanin), "A Feminist Response to Judge Lenehan's Ruling in the Trial of Al-Rawi" (MSVU Feminist Collective), and "The Blunt Instrument of the Law: Consent and HIV Non-Disclosure" (Patten and Symington). A fourth chapter, entitled "Curated Consultation and the Illusion of Inclusion in York University's Sexual Assault Policymaking Process" (Gray, Pin, and Cooper), critically examines the production of a university sexual assault policy. Finally, "Military Sexual Violence in Canada" (Eichler) argues that Canada's methods of training and deploying soldiers promote sexual assault within the military, and offers suggestions for change.

In the words of Armstrong and Bernstein (2008), "institutions are where ... classification systems are anchored and infused with material consequences" (83). Contributors to the section "Legislation, Policy, and Government" cast critical lenses on the institutions they examine. These authors focus on the "controlling, obligating, or inhibiting" (Martin 2004: 1251) mechanisms through which institutions "maintain order" (1253) and social inequalities.

Feminists since the second wave have been deeply engaged in discussions about relationships between sexual violence, consent, and the law. In the 18th-century Western world, "rape" meant theft of male property in the form of women's bodies (Smith 1999). Enslaved, racialized, and poor women whose sexualities were not valued as saleable property by those in power were legally "unrapeable." This legislation was itself an example of state sexualized violence against women's bodies, understood as property. State violence, as argued by Nicholas Blomley (2003), whether carried out by military, police, or the courts, is essential to any colonial nation state, since violence is necessary for the imposition of property and property laws. Once they are taken as natural, "the propertied divisions that force the poor into public space or women sex-trade workers into unsafe spaces disappear. Thus, the violence unleashed against such outlaws appears either as outside law itself ... or as a disinterested and objective policing of collective norms" (132).

Several contributors, including Patten and Symington, Gallant and Zanin, and the msvu Feminist Collective, have considered whose violence, whose victimization and/or whose consensual sex end up being considered sexual assault under current Canadian law, either as written or as applied. Hierarchies once written directly into law continue to distinguish legitimate from illegitimate victims in the popular and juridical imaginary and to decide who counts as a perpetrator of violence. These hierarchies are maintained through the systemic biases and economic inequalities that shape how and what police officers, prosecutors, defence lawyers, judges, and juries perceive.

Jeremy Duru (2004) makes this point in his investigation of the white mythology that frames Black men as sexually dangerous, a mythology that has the intent and effect of producing and legitimating anti-Black violence. In his words, "the substantial reforms following the Scottsboro tragedy did not protect the Central Park Five, so there is little reason to believe reforms instituted in the wake of the Central Park tragedy would necessarily protect the next group of black men falsely accused of rape" (21). So long as there is popular belief in the racist myth of the dangerous Black man, it "will continue to discover entries into the criminal justice system" (21). Sherene Razack (2000) has similarly demonstrated how white, colonial seeing produced the murder of Saulteaux mother Pamela George and then shaped the trial and ruling that followed it.

Dis/Consenting Agents

It has been suggested above that institutions produce many of the "material consequences" (Armstrong and Bernstein 2008: 83) of hierarchical social classification systems such as race, gender, dis/ability, and sexual orientation. As argued by Wilkerson, these categories are constructed in no small part through apportioning of sexual violence, sexual consent, and sexual persecution. Whereas the section "Legislation, Policy, and Government" includes chapters that focus critically on the operation of institutions with respect to sexual violence and sexual consent, "Dis/Consenting Agents" presents testimony of social agents who variously negotiate and resist structured and institutionalized negations of sexual autonomy. Three chapters included here are based on research participant testimony: "Surviving Woman-to-Woman Sexual Assault" (Malinen), "Power Struggles over the Sexualities of Individuals with Intellectual Disabilities in Alberta, Canada" (Santinele Martino), and "Sex Work and the Paradox of Consent" (Ralston). Two chapters are written from a first-person perspective: "What You Can Do, What You Can't Do, and What You're Going to Pay Me to Do It: A First-Person Account of Survival and Empowerment through Sex Work" (Paris Perry) and "Tender Places: On the Intersection of Anti-Rape Activism and Prison Abolitionism" (Jones and Whynacht).

In choosing the section title "Dis/Consenting Agents," I have in mind Loïc Wacquant's (2015) "social agent," who is theorized as "sentient, suffering, skilled, sedimented, and situated." As sentient, the agent is "capable of feeling and conscious of those feelings; and the body is the synthesizing medium of this feeling awareness." As suffering, she "has needs, yearnings, and desires that do not get fulfilled; she is constantly subjected to the judgement of others and faces the inescapable coming of death." As skilled, "the social agent can 'make a difference' ... because, through experience and training, she acquires capacities to act and the dexterity to do things competently." These elements are sedimented in that they are deposited "as the layered product of our varied individual and collective histories." Finally, the social agent is situated because this sediment forms in keeping with her social and physical locations; she "integrates the traces of the many places ... occupied over time" (3–4).

In many respects, the notion of the social agent is an apt vehicle for the chapters contained in this section. Her embodiment supports understanding sexual violence and consent as the embodied experiences they are. She is socially situated in a way that opens a window on questions each of these chapters might help readers to pursue, such as "How do embodied practices and skills inform individual and collective identities? How do stigmas and vulnerabilities shape embodied knowledges?" (Pitts-Taylor 2015: 21). The voices featured in this section draw on sedimented and embodied knowledge, situated in relation to social structures and institutions as they "make a difference" in a variety of registers.

CREATING SAFER CLASSROOMS
FOR ENGAGING WITH *DIS/CONSENT*

Texts such as this one, which include narratives of trauma-inducing situations and experiences, have a great deal to teach about social structures, institutions and experiences of diversely situated social agents. As evidenced in the pages of *Dis/Consent*, safe space is not distributed equitably in society. As discussed at length above, those with more social power are more likely to be safe from sexual violence and sexual stigmatization, whether structural, institutional, or interpersonal.

Dis/Consent may constitute emotionally difficult material for readers who have histories with related trauma as well as for readers who do not. Those "who have faced trauma in their pasts may revisit painful memories," while those without traumatic histories related to the text may experience "shattered assumptions" (McKenzie-Mohr 2004: 48).

Striving to create safe classroom space for students does not mean creating environments free of discomfort. Again, the pursuit of sexual liberation requires dialoguing about and from diverse perspectives. "To grow and learn, students often must confront issues that make them uncomfortable and force them to struggle with who they are and what they believe" (Holley and Steiner 2005: 50). Ideally, students become willing to take risks and encounter alternative framings as they share their views, knowledge, and experiences. In spaces that students define as safe, they report being "more likely to learn about others, to be challenged to expand their own viewpoints, to increase their self-awareness, and to develop effective communication skills" (58).

While risk is essential to learning, it is far more productive when students are "empowered to encounter risk on their own terms" (Hunter 2008, cited in The Roestone Collective 2014: 1355). Some professors find it useful to set ground rules or intentions for conversations with their students early in the term. Ground rules often include being respectful when challenging one another and giving one another the benefit of the doubt. In the words of The Roestone Collective (2014), "For scholars, activists, and scholar-activists, recognizing and negotiating social difference is crucial for building solidarities, substantively addressing questions of diversity, challenging the status quo, and doing intersectional activism or research" (1360).

Students can also be given freedom to individually negotiate, on their own terms, emotionally difficult course material. Instructors may wish to adapt some or all of the following statement, a version of which I include on most of my syllabi and discuss at the beginning of the term:

> As sociologists, we understand that our private troubles are interconnected with social structures. Throughout the semester, we will explore some issues that may, as a consequence of just such connections, be experienced as upsetting. For example, issues of violence, racism, colonialism, sexism and heterosexism will arise. Descriptions of sexual violence will appear in some of our readings. I encourage you to talk to me if you have concerns about the emotional impacts of reading about or discussing any of these themes in class. I invite you to look ahead in the syllabus, scan our readings and discuss any concerns with me.

Students who find that an area of course content poses emotional difficulty may request a special consideration without being asked to share the reasons for their requests. Examples of considerations include the following:

- a decision that the student should not read a given text (e.g., in the past I have allowed a student to exchange a particular chapter for another reading),
- a decision that a particular material should be avoided in lecture (e.g., in the past I have removed a film on abortion from in-class viewing and made it optional at-home material),
- a reminder that the student is always free to leave class if experiencing feelings of distress, and
- a decision that the student may choose not to attend the class meeting on a specific day.

Note that students are always free to step out of class, and counselling services are available on campus.

As specified in the statement I put on my syllabi, I do not ask students who request accommodation related to disturbing content for personal information about why a reading or film feels too difficult. To do so would be inconsistent with principles of trauma-informed practice. In the time I have been providing students with statements such as the one above, I have never doubted the legitimacy of a student's request. In most classes, I receive no requests for special consideration related to emotionally difficult material. Occasionally, students who have not requested any accommodation have nonetheless reported feeling safer because the difficult nature of the content had been recognized and special considerations offered. Moreover, a statement such as this helps to remind us of the profound interconnections between the personal and the political — between the structures and institutions that appear in *Dis/Consent* and our experiences as social agents.

CONCLUSION

Dis/Consent resists the heteropatriarchal and colonial status quo that produces and justifies oppression through negation of sexual autonomy. Because misogyny, sexism, heteronormativity, racism, classism, and ableism are deeply intertwined with sexual violence, sexual violence will not be undone in the absence of systemic, anti-oppressive, decolonizing change. This volume aspires to generate important conversations about sexual violence and sexual consent, and ultimately to support imaginings of (sexually) non-violent cultures.

Chapter 2

OPENING

Beginnings and Renewal, Oppression and Fragmentation

Sherry Pictou

Sexual violence and other forms of violence have been disproportionately perpetrated against Indigenous women and girls since the beginning of Canadian colonialism. Indeed, the violent targeting of Indigenous women and girls has its roots in colonial processes. And yet, the position of victim so often imagined for our women and girls does not speak to our existence within a culture that is very much alive.

In this chapter, I offer a revised and condensed version of some of the chapters written for my MA thesis, which was based on the perspectives of eight Mi'kmaw women employed in First Nations organizations within their communities. The thesis, entitled "The Life Experiences and Personal Transformations of Mi'kmaq Women," was completed in 1996 — the same year that the *Report of the Royal Commission on Aboriginal Peoples* high-lighted violence against Indigenous women and their children. Twenty years later this violence continues unabated; both the voices of the eight Mi'kmaw women I interviewed and quote here and the recommendations of the Royal Commission remain perfectly relevant to this volume on dis/consent.

Failure to address intersections of social, cultural, economic, and political forms of oppression against Indigenous women not only supports the continuation of gendered violence against us but also compromises Indigenous efforts at decolonization. Those treaty and land claim negotiations that courts have compelled settler society to undertake tend to be state driven and focused on unsustainable neoliberal resource extraction as a form of economic development. Hence, these processes extend or renew colonialism (Alfred and Corntassel 2005; Barker 2009; Pictou 2017; Tuck and McKenzie 2015). Gendered tensions are playing out in Mi'kma'ki and around the world, as Indigenous women take central roles in struggles to protect access to food, land, and water from corporate and political interests (Altamirano-Jimenez 2013; Gies 2015). Strong parallels and deep interconnections exist between the dispossession of Indigenous Peoples of their ancestral homelands, environmental degradation under the settler state, and violence against Indigenous women and girls. This chapter argues that decolonization requires eradication of discrimination and violence against Indigenous women and children and a reclaiming of women's roles in food and lifeways.

DESCRIPTION OF OPENING AND CLOSING CHAPTERS

There are various Indigenous teachings and interpretations about the four directions of East, South, West, and North.[1] These directions represent the cyclical seasons, the process of sunrise to sunset, the stages of human development, and animal teachings, among many more. The four quadrant directions frame the two chapters I have written to bookend *Dis/Consent* with an Indigenous woman's lens on sexual violence and resistance. This first chapter focuses on the directions of East and West, while the last chapter focuses on North and South. Together, the chapters represent the intersection of two paths or the intersection of all the cardinal points indicated by the ancestral Mi'kmaw eight-pointed star (Pictou 2017; Young 2016). East represents the beginnings and renewal of Mi'kmaw women's knowledge and experience, while West represents the oppression and fragmentation of Mi'kmaw women's knowledge and experience. North represents how Mi'kmaw women have survived colonial oppression, and South represents the essence of Mi'kmaw women's resilience, a resurgence of nurturing and growth generated by establishing sacred relationships with all of life, including with allies.

EAST (BEGINNINGS AND RENEWAL)

East is the direction where we find the promise of renewal, with each spring season generating new growth (Hampton 1993, 1995). It is in this direction we find our beginnings and the process for our continued renewal as Mi'kmaw women and as Mi'kmaw People. Our worldview evolves from our consciousness of the whole universe as comprised of living, eternal, moving forces. It involves intricate and complex inter-relationships between our language, culture, individual and group relationships, and relationships with nature and land.

Our Mi'kmaw consciousness begins with giving birth and our mothering processes in the context of being women and our relationship with Mother Earth. Many of our ceremonial practices today are based on these principles and are where we find our beginnings. As Mi'kmaw women we are conscious of how we ourselves are givers of life. Giving life is a transformational process for us, where we recognize our strengths in ourselves and with our children. Ann, one of the Mi'kmaw women I interviewed, reflected, "My strengths are my children. They have always been my strength and they are still today, and they have expanded to my grandchildren. And I'm more stronger."

Collectively as Mi'kmaw People, we traditionally recognized the trans-formative process of giving birth and mothering by celebrating new life and the raising of children as a sacred honour: "The child would be right in the centre, and the dance would be circling around the child.... And that's the way they give these full thanks of this child.... [note that he then sings]" (Chief William Paul to Dr. Helen Creighton. Taped interview, Shubenacadie, Nova Scotia, 1944. Whitehead 1991: 222–223).

Recognizing ourselves as givers of life is also transformative in the sense that our mothering brings meaning and influences life decisions; where we decide to live depends on where our children and grandchildren can learn their language and culture. Just as significant, our ancestral understand-ings teach us that birthing processes interrelate with the generation of all living forces within the universe, which is premised on the interrelation-ship of Mother Earth and the Father Sun or Light (Henderson, Marshall, and Alfred 1993). Some other feminists also understand mothering as a "life-affirming" (Hart 1992: 201) transformative learning process that also relates to "human dependence on nature" (202–203).

Mi'kmaw women consider these interrelationships a sacred part of mothering. As one interviewee said,

> As a Mi'kmaw woman, for me the importance is my language as a Native person.... And I always taught my children to respect water, trees, and animals. Never abuse animals and food. I always tell my kids that when we put food out, it is important that it never goes to waste because there are little animals and little birds going around hungry. And I know how it feels to go hungry as a little kid and as an adult. (Maria)

Murdena Marshall, a respected Mi'kmaw woman and Elder, as well as a former Mi'kmaw professor at the University of Cape Breton, explains how in our language everything is either animate or inanimate. All that is animate is life and is perceived as including our relations with each other and with "all of creation — anything that grows" (Field notes, June 1995). Those of us who have lost the language or never learned to speak it fluently feel something missing. However, we continue to rely on our teachings, rooted in land- and water-based practices for food and lifeways, to guide us in our life journeys. These practices nurture our consciousness and our identity on individual and tribal/collective levels simultaneously. We express our identities in terms of pride and strength:

> I will never lose that [pride], because I was born an Indian and I will die as an Indian woman! (Maria)

> It's my identity. My culture and language is my identity. It makes me who I am and I'm proud of that. I am proud to be able to speak my language and understand it, and I can relate to my people. (Monica)

Within our Mi'kmaw community, we express a sense of belonging:

> It's important just to socialize within the community on the same level and you know, just a feeling of belonging to somewhere.... You either have a sense of belonging or your sense of, I'd say, security. (Beonka)

> I would never leave it [Mi'kmaw community] … because I was
> brought up here, this is my family, this whole community is mine.
> I could say I belong there. (Mary)

Our individual and tribal consciousness and our identity as Indigenous and Mi'kmaw women is intricately tied to a sense of belonging in Indigenous communities (Allen 1992; Ermine 1995; Henderson et al. 1993), which is found in the teachings of the East.

WEST (OPPRESSION AND FRAGMENTATION)

West is symbolic of the season of autumn, when all the trees shed their leaves and the grasses turn brown. It is a time for preparing for the coming of snow and winter storms. Eber Hampton (1993: 283) describes West as representing the process of European "conquest" and "invasion," or what Indigenous scholars argue is ongoing colonialism. In this context, Mi'kmaw People borrow the direction of West to mark our experiences of oppression with settler colonialism and how these experiences continue to intersect and disrupt our Eastern beginnings of who we are. These intersections inform our ongoing struggle to develop and maintain relationships with all living forces.

West represents the imposition of colonial concepts of civilization, an imposition that has caused a lot of frustration and confusion for our ancestors and for today's generation, in particular for our generation of Indigenous women. Religious, educational, political, and economic policies enforcing the dislocation of our mothering processes of women and earth have been reinforced by the Indian Act of 1876. The Indian Act is an invasion of our culture and our homes (Monture-Angus 1995). It has legislated our exclusion from tribal government, dispossession of land, patriarchal marriage, confinement to reserves, displacement from reserves, revocation of our status, and seizure of our children. Patriarchy invades our Mi'kmaw consciousness through colonialism and fragments the totality of our experience and our sense of identity in various ways. As Mi'kmaw women we have grown up through childhood learning experiences characterized by racism and sexism. We experience these forms of oppression as adults, and as mothers whose children also experience racism and sexism.

Paula Gunn Allen (1992: 41) states that the first objective of colonialism is transforming tribal societies into hierarchal and patriarchal ones by "displacing the female as creator with male-gendered creators." Fundamental to colonial ideologies of civilization are dominating religious concepts of a noun-god (he) that is separate from humans and from the earth or nature. Land/earth is conceived of as property to be acquired and exploited for capital gain or profit. Property ownership is continuous with Western patriarchal notions of male entitlement to women's bodies. On the other hand, property ownership runs counter to Indigenous worldviews and practices. The Mi'kmaq migrated with the availability of food resources dictated by the seasons (Henderson et al. 1993; Pictou 2017; see also Allen 1992) until colonialism dispossessed them of their ancestral homelands, isolating them on reserves and seizing the land and nature as property. Not having access to our ancestral land disrupts and fragments the land-based practices that nurture our consciousness and our reciprocal relationships with each other and with the earth (Allen 1992; Deloria 1994; Henderson et al. 1993; Monture-Angus 1995).

Unlike European society, our communities were not patriarchal, patrilineal, or patrilocal. Rather, particularly in the southern part of Nova Scotia, many of our marriages were bilocal, meaning that married couples had the option to live with the family and community of either the man or woman (Wicken 1994: 124–128). An indication that Mi'kmaw communities were not always patriarchal can be found as recently as 1921, when Jerry Lonecloud stated, "Our wives don't like to be called after their husbands … they don't like to get into white ways" (To Clara Dennis, Scrapbook No. 1, 1923. Public Archives of Nova Scotia. Whitehead, 1991: 323). Hence, a second mode of disruption was initiated through the imposition of European concepts of marriage (and a noun-god) that involved naming and identifying our people through patrilineal baptism and matrimony. No longer would we identify our relationships and ourselves with all living forces of the universe like my female ancestors did with names such as One Who Likes to Stand in The Wind, or Flower of the Woods.

A third disruption was initiated through the imposition of European economic roles for men and women. Having isolated us on reserves, colonial actors interrupted our physical and spiritual contributions to land-based subsistence survival with policies that forced men into agricultural production and women into household activities. This displaced Mi'kmaw women from our central roles in securing and preparing foods, roles that were traditionally considered sacred. In residential schools and day schools established on the reserves, Indigenous boys and girls (sometimes siblings) were forcibly separated and taught to perform working-class economic roles considered gender-appropriate by settler society. Our children were made to observe the noun-god while being sexually, physically, and spiritually molested by priests and nuns. These institutions were intended to eradicate the Mi'kmaw language, an effort in many ways carried on by the current education system. The greatest disruption to our consciousness was the severing of our mothering from our children's (intergenerational) learning.

In an interview, Charlotte recalled painfully the feelings of abandonment, isolation, and racism that ran through her experience of being removed from her family and placed in a residential school:

> And then we were in the ball field, we were in the ball field on our way home … three men come and picked us up.… They said, "Come on, we're going to take you to this nice place and you're going to get lots to eat and you'll get clothes." And they gave you this nice bright shiny picture, and I was really happy to go. And once I got there [Shubenacadie Residential School] it reminded me of a prison.… Well I learned not to speak Micmac.[2] That was beat out of me.… You were beat [pause] with a leather strap. It was something like what you sharpened razor blades with or knives with at butcher stores. I remember one time they beat me and beat me and beat me for stealing something, and I never stole. And I kept saying, "No, I didn't. No, I didn't. I didn't. I didn't steal!" But they keep beating me and beating me. And the only way I could get them to stop, I had to say, "Yes, I stole." Yet I didn't [pause].

Other Mi'kmaw women also recalled being physically beaten for speaking their language in day school:

> Yes … I could never trust non-Native people, because when I started to go to school I could not understand non-Native

language. I only understood my own language. And I used to get beaten if I wanted to use the washroom, but I didn't know how to say it in English. It was so intimidating I would say because sometimes I use to piss myself because the teacher wouldn't let me go to the washroom.... I didn't know how to say it. (Maria)

[Being] brought up by my grandparents ... they would speak the language. When I started school, I can remember getting beaten because I spoke Micmac. I didn't understand any English. I couldn't speak any English. (Monica)

Those of us who attended public schools during the 1960s also experienced racism as children. We continue to experience racism in higher institutions of learning from both professors and non-Mi'kmaw students.

I took this course.... I don't know why, but I took it. And the professor described, she said, "A typical native community was a community that ... was poor sanitation conditions, housing conditions," and she was just going on and on, you know. (Beonka)

While there are statistics that underscore how many Indigenous People, especially Indigenous women and children, continue to live in poverty and poor housing conditions in Canada (Anaya 2014), portraying Indigenous communities only through poverty obscures how poverty is systematically related to gendered racism. It further obscures how the Mi'kmaw community offers Mi'kmaw women a sense of belonging and informs our struggle or agency to survive against the patriarchal structures imposed in our communities, as discussed in the closing chapter (see also Pictou 2017).

These patriarchal structures force us into subservient roles. Marrying non-Indigenous men made us culturally and sexually subservient to the mainstream patriarchal order. If we chose not to marry, then our children were labelled illegitimate.

I was well known for fighting with the boys at school. Well ... they kept calling me *squaw*. And it wasn't till years later when I started working at a restaurant ... they [men] would be sitting out there and waiting and they would say, "Let's go up to squaw road!" … Then [to] one of the other workers there, I said, "What are they talking about, squaw road?"… Their [the men's] attitude was, "We'll go up there and get a piece of ass." We'll put it that way. Because there were other Native women that lived there, and some had what is called illegitimate children.… "Just another Indian woman" — that was their attitude. (Little Bird)

In 1985 the government attempted to address gender discrimination in the Indian Act, which had stripped status from Indigenous women who married non-Indigenous men, by reinstating status for these women through Bill C-31 (Palmater 2011). However, reinstatement extended only to the first and second generations.[3] This is what Susan was referring to in an interview when she spoke about how her daughter could lose status:

[Under] the Indian Act … a Micmac woman would be banned from the reserve if you married a non-Native. You were kicked off the reserve. There's still that discrimination like, say even with my daughter, if she marries a non-Native and has a child, then her daughter loses her status.

Colonial forms of patriarchy further serve to transform our sense of who we are to the point where we start to internalize our own oppression:

Many of the rules developed [that were supposed] to protect Indians are now used by Indians against Indians, particularly against Indian women. This is an indication that the colonized have accepted their colonization. As a result of the internalization of colonization, the colonizer can step back from the devastation caused by their acts. (Monture-Angus 1995: 135)

Indigenous men, in particular, are rewarded with individual economic materialism and positions of power for becoming assimilated (Allen 1992; hooks 1988; Monture-Angus, 1995; Satzewich and Wotherspoon, 1993). Nowhere is this more evident than in the transformation of our ancestral governance structures into ones that are male-centred and controlled and funded by the state through the imposition of Indian Act elections of chiefs and councils. Indigenous women were excluded from voting or running for elected positions up until 1951 (Walls 2010). And though there are more elected Indigenous women, the Indigenous male dominance in land claim and treaty negotiations and in political organizations such as the Assembly of First Nations is still overwhelmingly prevalent (Borrows 2013; Monture-Angus 1995). Tragically, this also translates into various forms of physical, sexual, and mental violence against women and children (Allen 1992; Monture-Angus 1995), which coincide with the dispossession of our natural sources of food and lifeways (Jacobs 2013; Women's Earth Alliance and Native Youth Sexual Health Network n.d.)

Indigenous women across Canada continue to struggle against extended and renewed settler-colonial oppression marked by the federal government's ongoing refusal to fully address gender discrimination in the Indian Act of 1876. Under this act, countless Indigenous women — along with their children — have lost their status by marrying non-Indigenous men. While the exact number of Indigenous women who lost status is not known, government reports estimate somewhere from 80,000 to 2 million Indigenous People would be entitled to status if gender discrimination were fully removed from the Indian Act (Galloway 2017). Further, not only did the Royal Commission on Aboriginal Peoples highlight violence against Indigenous women and their children, it also drew attention to poor living conditions facing Indigenous communities and the gender discrimination of the Indian Act.

Almost twenty years later, in 2014, the United Nations' *Report of the Special Rapporteur on the Rights of Indigenous Peoples: The Situation of Indigenous Peoples in Canada* drew attention to the issue of missing and murdered Indigenous women and emphasized ongoing issues of poor living conditions and family violence, which finds its roots in the colonial patriarchal structures reinforced in Indigenous societies. In addition to refusing to truly address gender discrimination, the federal government also refuses to redress the fact that Indigenous children living on reserve do not receive the same level of children and family services as children living off reserve, as identified in 2015 by the government's own Canadian Human Rights Tribunal.

Also in 2015, the Truth and Reconciliation Commission released its calls to action, outlining recommendations on how government and education systems could address the impacts of residential school, including family and domestic violence. It called on the government "to appoint a public inquiry into the causes of, and remedies for, the disproportionate victimization of Aboriginal women and girls" (4). The inquiry has since been appointed but has progressed slowly in its mission, with a number of appointees resigning due to internal differences (Hui 2017). Meanwhile, Indigenous women and girls go missing or are violently murdered at four times the rate of other women in settler Canada (Borrows 2013). Canadian settler colonialism has both caused and benefited from sexual and other forms of violence against Indigenous women and girls and, more broadly, from erosion of the status of Indigenous women both within and outside of their communities. This is because women have long played foundational roles in maintaining Indigenous food and lifeways that by their very existence resist neoliberal economics.

In this context, the most painful aspects in expressing our learning experiences as Mi'kmaw women involve recalling inner conflict about who we are within cycles of physical, sexual, and psychological abuse; addictions; and child abuse. As Mi'kmaw women we learned how to develop alcoholism from our experiences with our parents' alcoholism, developed by our parents to numb their pain. We often turned to alcohol and drug abuse to numb our own pain as children and as women:

> I was always searching and the only thing, the only reason why I drank … it wasn't because, to be happy, to have fun, to go to dances. The only reason why I drank was to forget the pain, to numb the pain I was feeling: the pain of loneliness, the pain [of] abandonment. (Ann)

> I think today that we carry so many problems, and when we turn to alcohol or drugs we numb ourselves. We cover our feelings, we don't feel, we're numb. So I would call it [an] easier, softer way of dealing with things. Because I remember when I drank, I turned numb. I don't feel. (Maria)

When the addiction failed to numb the pain, and as we lost our way back to our inner selves, our wish for physical death to end the pain became overwhelming:

> I contemplated it [suicide]. There were times I would come out

here and sit in the front room after he [spouse] would come home, sexually abuse me, physically abuse me. And ... at that time ... I had a revolver. And I would load it up and sit on the couch.... To me there were people who would pray to God that they would live tomorrow. Here I was praying to God that he would take me and I wouldn't see tomorrow. I knew what is in tomorrow. (Monica)

My sexual abuse as a child ... I couldn't understand why that happened to me. Why my stepfather did that to me.... And that is why I left home [at the age of fifteen] and married.... That's how I got out of there. But things did not change.... Mental abuse, sexual abuse, and physical abuse.... I call it today sexual abuse because the things he [spouse] did to me, today I know they were not right. (Maria)

Despite all of this, the women of our communities have never stopped resisting. To date, any progress in securing the legal rights of Indigenous women has been due to the advocacy and agency of Indigenous women themselves. Building on the advocacy of Mary Two-Axe Earley, several legal challenges against the Indian Act were initiated. These challenges resulted in Bill C-31, passed in 1985, which reinstated status for women and children who had lost it through marriage, as discussed above. However, this did not apply to grandchildren. More recently, Dr. Lynn Gehl and her lawyer Christa Big Canoe successfully challenged the remaining gender discrimination against grandchildren of women whose status had been revoked (Aboriginal Legal Services 2017). However, Bill C-3, drafted to address these continued shortcomings, is still limited in the sense that proof of status through lineage can only be traced back to 1951, the year that registration of Indigenous Peoples was created (Galloway 2017). This is not an issue for men (Galloway 2017). Gender discrimination within the Indian Act predates 1951 considerably: the Gradual Civilization Act of 1857 required males over the age of 21 who could read or write, and by extension their wives, to enfranchise as subjects of the British Crown. Under the Indian Act of 1876, an Indigenous woman who married an Indigenous man not from her community (band) was legally required to transfer to her husband's band (Palmater 2011). If she married a non-Indigenous man, she would then lose her status altogether. In other words, non-Indigenous-male dominance became the criterion for assimilation. Indigenous men who could read or write like their non-Indigenous male counterparts, and Indigenous women who married non-Indigenous men, would forcibly become Canadian. These colonial patriarchal standards are continuously translated into legal mechanisms for oppressing and extinguishing the existence of thousands of Indigenous People, and Indigenous women, in particular.

Almost 150 years since the inauguration of the Gradual Civilization Act, despite the release of several high-profile reports calling for remedial action, gender discrimination against Indigenous women remains enshrined in Canadian colonial law. The United Nations Human Rights Committee recently declared that the Indian Act continues to discriminate against First Nations women. The erasure of Indigenous existence through gender discrimination intricately intersects with current land claim and treaty negotiation processes through which colonial actors aim to dispossess Indigenous Peoples of their ancestral homelands in exchange for the promise of economic development. These multilayered patriarchal constructions continue to dislocate our knowledge and lifeways for survival, which are informed by our ancestral homelands. Patricia Monture-Angus (1995) describes our experiences of external oppression and internalized oppression as both physical and psychological violence rooted in colonial patriarchy. Therefore, fundamental to strategies for decolonization is the examination of violence against Indigenous women and girls through the lens of colonialism as well as patriarchy. Some of these strategies that evolve out of Mi'kmaw women's experience are explored in the closing chapter.

PART I

LEGISLATION, POLICY, AND GOVERNMENT

Chapter 3

THE BOGUS BDSM DEFENCE

The Manipulation of Kink
as Consent to Assault

Chanelle Gallant and Andrea Zanin

In psychiatry, the media, the law, and various streams of feminism, consensual BDSM (bondage, discipline, sadism, and masochism) has often been conflated with assault, especially with violence against women. This conflation has led to the punishment of consensual BDSM, where judges have refused to believe women's claims of enthusiastic consent even when no party is claiming any harm, injury, or force. For example, in *Smith v. Smith* (2003), a woman who had engaged in consensual kinky sex lost custody of her child and was court-ordered to undergo mandatory psychotherapy sessions for "domestic violence." Her consent to kinky sex was taken as "proof of mental incompetence" (Khan 2014: 287).

This problematic treatment comes in part out of a failure to recognize the validity and significance of women's sexual consent. As kinky feminists who understand that BDSM can be profoundly positive for women, we are disturbed by the paternalistic, sexist idea that women cannot meaningfully consent to non-normative sex.

In the last five years, however, two men in high-profile Canadian trials, accused of assault in one case and homicide in the other, have mobilized consensual BDSM as a defence. We see no reason to believe that any of the victims in these cases consented — or were invited to consent — to BDSM play, and we are troubled by the use of what we refer to in this chapter as the bogus BDSM defence, used by men accused of sexually assaulting or murdering women.

In 2014, media personality Jian Ghomeshi was accused of battering and sexually assaulting multiple women and was fired by the CBC. In his initial public comments, he attempted to explain his actions as BDSM play, claiming he was being subjected to an attack on kinky sex.[1] By the time of his trial, Ghomeshi had dropped this defence entirely. He was found not guilty in 2016.

In 2015, Bradley Barton went to trial for the murder of Cindy Gladue. The medical examiner testified that Gladue had died of blood loss from an injury caused by a sharp object. Barton admitted to causing the wound but testified that no weapon was used and that her death was the accidental result of consensual "rough sex." He was found not guilty of any charges in 2015. After an enormous public outcry, where thousands of Canadians protested, the prosecutor announced the case would be retried.

Though the Ghomeshi and Barton cases are quite different, both men were accused of severe, non-consensual harm and force and argued that they should be exonerated because the women had consented to BDSM. Why was Barton able to convince a jury that consensual BDSM exonerated him of any legal wrongdoing, whereas Ghomeshi had dropped any mention of BDSM by the time his case got to court?

We acknowledge that men are not the only people capable of committing violence or consent violations. We do not wish to reproduce the heterosexism of anti-BDSM arguments in our own analysis. Nonetheless, the cases we analyze involve male violence against women, and we have shaped the focus of this article accordingly.

Also, while we focus on legal cases, this should not be interpreted as reflecting a belief in the capacity of the criminal legal system to prevent sexual violence or to bring healing and justice to survivors through its reform. The criminal legal system is one of the institutional pillars of settler colonialism, white supremacy, and patriarchy, and we examine it for what it *reflects* about dominant society's stance on sexual violence, not as the site for *solutions* to sexual violence.

In this essay, we use an intersectional feminist and kink-positive lens to consider under what circumstances contemporary kink-positive discourse about BDSM and consent can be manipulated to obscure responsibility for assault — and how some feminists play into that manipulation. We argue that the outcomes of these cases were differently shaped by the intersection of public acceptance and public ignorance regarding BDSM and consent as well as by the relative impacts of white privilege, colonialism, and respectability. The circumstances, details, and implications of the two cases are very different, and a comprehensive analysis is beyond the scope of this essay; we focus here on analyzing how BDSM was employed as a defence tactic by the accused men.

CONSENT IN BDSM

BDSM is a hybrid abbreviation standing for bondage, discipline, dominance, submission, sadism, and masochism. BDSM and kink involve the consensual use of power, often eroticized, in the form of negotiated roles; pain, in the sense of intense physical sensation; and/or fetish objects or practices for the pleasure of all concerned (Zanin 2010: 64–68).

In his work on consent in BDSM, Robin Bauer (2014: 76) argues that the law in many countries embraces a liberal notion of consent, framing it as a "sexual contract set up by free individuals," and that BDSM communities often adopt a similar stance. In contrast, he writes, "some lesbian feminists oppose this idea, pointing out that women especially have been socialized into consenting to male dominance in a patriarchal culture. Therefore, even if a woman consents to dominance, this does not mean she does so of her own free will" (76).

The problem with this particular approach is that if we are waiting to achieve perfect social equality before consent from women and other marginalized groups is deemed valid, we are effectively stripping these groups of the right to consent — sexually or otherwise.[2] As kinky feminists, we believe women who say they were sexually assaulted, and we also believe women who assert their consent. We recognize that women's consent to BDSM is valid and meaningful, while also recognizing that social hierarchies of oppression shape women's lives and choices. Clearly we need a more nuanced model capable of holding these two realities simultaneously.

To this end, Bauer argues for "critical consent," where "actors do not need to be equal (which is practically impossible), but do need to be able to access negotiating power in that particular situation" (106). In other words, rather than focusing entirely on overarching systems of oppression as the sole determiners of the validity of consent, we need to assess consent in individual situations, taking interpersonal and situational factors into account and, as a baseline, believe women's own assessments of their desires and negotiating power. Bauer writes that in BDSM, consent is "negotiated, affective and critical" and defines it as "an active, ongoing collaboration for the mutual benefit of all involved, helping to establish and maintain each participant's own sense of integrity" (106). In practice, BDSM communities provide a plethora of tools for negotiating consent, including an emphasis on explicit verbal communication, checklists, safe words and safe signals, check-ins, contracts, consideration of aftercare needs, and many more.[3] Further, Bauer argues that such an understanding of consent "leads to an ethics of heightened responsibility and accountability for the consequences of one's actions as well as to a sense of increased sexual agency ... not based on an ignorance of social hierarchies or norms" (106).

While the practice of BDSM does not intrinsically guarantee good negotiation skills, the premise of BDSM consent negotiation has been held up in recent scholarship as a model for negotiations in all kinds of sexual relationships (see Kleinplatz 2006: 325–347). This premise lies in stark contrast to the situations described by complainants in the Ghomeshi case and evidenced in the Barton trial.

MISPERCEPTIONS ABOUT BDSM

In some legal, psychiatric, and feminist discourses, BDSM is often assumed to involve less consent, or less valid consent, than vanilla sex. For example, in their written statement to the Alberta appeal court requesting that Barton be retried, the Women's Legal Education and Action Fund (LEAF) and Institute for the Advancement of Aboriginal Women (2017) stigmatized BDSM and displaced responsibility for assault away from perpetrators and onto BDSM practice. These organizations explicitly equated BDSM with harm:

> With one exception, we reject the proposition that when someone consents to engage in sexual activity, whether for payment

or otherwise, that necessarily includes consent to bodily harm or even the risk of bodily harm. The one exception is for those individuals who engage in sexual activity with a view to causing or risking bodily harm, as in sado-masochistic sex. (52)

A blanket exception on bodily harm for BDSM may on its surface seem kink-positive, but in fact is no more helpful than blanket condemnation of BDSM practices. Neither position considers the factors that inform an individual's access to negotiation power and consent, or the basic care and safety measures required for all sex and BDSM. In keeping with our own experience, contemporary research on kinky communities shows kinky people often expect a high standard of consent, including explicit negotiations about desired activities and limits (see Weiss 2011: 80–83). In contrast, because heterosexual vanilla sex is normative, shoddy or absent negotiation is often unremarked, naturalized, or even romanticized. It is possible to commit assault within BDSM, because the simple fact of being kinky or being part of BDSM communities does not guarantee adequate consent practice. As such we do not define BDSM as being somehow exempt from the possibility of assault. We do, however, insist that BDSM is not by definition assault and has no inherent connection or semblance to assault, in the same way that sex is not by definition rape. The question of consent is key at all times in all types of human interaction.

Furthermore, the risks of BDSM tend to be exaggerated or poorly understood by non-practitioners, while the dangers of vanilla sex (especially heterosexual) are minimized.[4] For example, 30 percent of women report regularly experiencing unwanted pain during vaginal intercourse, and 72 percent of women experience unwanted pain from anal intercourse (Herbenick et al. 2015).[5] Many women suffer preventable sex-related injuries, including vaginal and anal tearing, largely caused by a lack of arousal and lubricant, to say nothing of sexually transmitted infection risks, which are not present in many BDSM practices. Common BDSM activities such as spanking, bondage, and the like often do not involve genital contact or bodily fluids and thus carry no risk of STI transmission. Yet heterosexual intercourse is seen as a less risky sexual activity than BDSM because women's unwanted suffering for male pleasure is normalized (see Loofbourow 2018).

Holding men responsible for assault requires destigmatizing kinky sex and kinky women. It also requires unambiguously asserting that women can consent to kink without consenting to assault. Arguing that consent to BDSM is consent to damage and harm can obscure the responsibility for genuine harm by displacing it onto kinky sex itself. Put another way, when we misunderstand kinky sex as necessarily non-consensual and extremely dangerous, and we misunderstand kinky women as providing blanket consent to all violence and risk, it becomes possible to make a case that victims have consented to assault or murder simply by framing them as kinky. This device can be successful regardless of whether the women in question self-identify as kinky. Most disturbingly, it can also succeed when the women are no longer alive to speak for themselves.

The cases we highlight here show this displacement of responsibility is being invoked to defend against accusations of violence that bear no resemblance to BDSM practice as we know it.

THE BOGUS BDSM DEFENCE

BDSM currently occupies an ambivalent place in public discourse. While older ideas about pathology remain active, we are also seeing an unprecedented level of kink-positive representation in popular culture. The popularity of kink-related cultural products such as the *Fifty Shades of Grey* books and films has had both positive and negative effects on public discourse about kink: Society may be more accepting of kink than ever before, but that acceptance does not necessarily equate to a deeper understanding of critical consent.[6] This vulnerable spot in the public imagination, where goodwill intersects with ignorance, is ripe for exploitation by individuals wishing to defend non-consensual sexual behaviour by using the language of BDSM. Here we critically examine two recent Canadian legal cases in which the bogus BDSM defence was part of the overall narrative.

The Murder of Cindy Gladue

Cindy Gladue of Edmonton, Alberta, was a 36-year-old Indigenous woman, a sex worker, an eldest daughter, and the mother of three teenage girls. Bradley Barton stood accused of her murder in 2015. We make two intersecting arguments about this trial. First, we believe discrimination against Indigenous women and sex workers in Canada explains much about how Gladue became the first person in Canadian legal history whose killing was excused, in large part, on the basis of the defendant's claim that he and the victim had been engaged in consensual kinky sex. Second, we believe that fundamental misapprehensions about kinky sex enabled the success of this claim. We first address the misunderstandings of kink that appeared in the trial, and then address the question of discrimination against Indigenous women and sex workers.

Misperceptions of BDSM in the Barton Trial

Jurors in the Barton trial showed an astonishingly skewed understanding of both kinky sexual practices and consent when they uncritically accepted consensual "rough sex" as an explanation for Gladue's death. The sexual act Barton claimed to have performed consensually with Gladue, known as "fisting," involves inserting a hand into a person's vagina or anus. When intervening in the Gladue case, LEAF and the Institute for the Advancement of Aboriginal Women fed into the presentation of fisting as a violent practice by objecting that the very use of this term "conveyed to the jury a normalization of this sexual activity" that caused "damage," "harm and pain" (53).[7] From our perspective as BDSM educators, it would take a profound misunderstanding of kinky sex to believe that fisting itself could lead to death. While a common practice in some spheres of BDSM because of the intense sensations it can provide, fisting is far from rough. In fact, it is typically slow and gentle; practitioners file their fingernails and use lots of lubricant for comfort and safety (see Sloane 2012: 69–86). According to Carol Queen (2004: 70), fisting "is not a process that one person does to another, it's something two people do together. The woman who's being penetrated gets to decide how fast, how far, how much, and she tells her partner these things." Like all sex, fisting involves some physical risk, but it rarely causes injury; the experts consulted in the Barton trial confirmed this (Hudson 2015). An accurate understanding of fisting would have left jurors unconvinced that this practice could explain Gladue's injuries, let alone result in death.

The evidence of Gladue's intoxication and Barton's failure to seek medical assistance only show further that this was not a case of consensual BDSM practice. When we consider the systems of oppression under which Gladue lived, including colonialism, racism, poverty, sexism, and substance addiction and criminalization, we can speculate that her access to negotiating power was very likely constrained or even nullified — though in the absence of her testimony, we cannot state this categorically. However, we can state categorically that she did not consent to her own death and that a legal decision that would enshrine such consent as possible is deeply troubling.

Anti-Indigenous Racism in the Barton Trial

Anti-Indigenous racism rests in part on a specific sexualization of Indigenous People by the Canadian colonial state and settlers. Indigenous People, particularly women, are constructed in the settler imagination as having uncivilized, "savage" bodies and sexualities that are always already dangerously out of bounds (Smith 2005; Sayers 2013). Indeed, the first anti-prostitution laws in Canada appeared in the Indian Act (Sayers 2013). The criminalization of Indigenous women as sex workers (or suspected sex workers) is deployed to justify control over Indigenous movement as well as state and interpersonal violence.

Gladue is one of the thousands of missing or murdered Indigenous women in Canada. Her murder is one part of the centuries-long assault by white settlers on Indigenous People's lands, families, nations, and bodies against their consent. In the white settler cultural and legal imagination, Indigenous People's consent is always violable — how else could the settler population still occupy this land? — and to be Indigenous and a sex worker is seen as consent to the risk of fatal violence (Hunt and Sayers 2015). In turn, this systemic violence maintains the conditions for ongoing land theft and resource extractivism.

When Barton stood trial for murder, court transcripts show that Gladue's sex work was mentioned at least twenty-six times; her Indigeneity was brought up twenty-five times (LEAF and Institute for the Advancement of Aboriginal Women 2017: 29). According to Ridgen (2017), "Gladue's sexual history was bantered around the courtroom.… She was frequently referred to as 'the prostitute' and 'the Native girl' by lawyers in the case." In a continuation of the horrific indifference Barton had shown Gladue's humanity, the courtroom saw her dismembered vagina as evidence — which is unprecedented in Canadian legal history (*National Post* 2015;

see also *R. v. Barton* 2015). While Gladue's treatment is unprecedented in Canadian law, it is part of a wider pattern of the way that settler legal systems treat Indigenous People's bodies with extreme disregard. Gladue's case recalls how in 1976, FBI agents in the U.S. ordered that the hands of murdered Native American activist Annie May Aquash be cut off and sent away for identification (see Kelley 1995).

We argue that the ultimate verdict of not guilty was shaped by a colonialist lens that presented an Indigenous woman sex worker as conceivably consenting to anything, including brutal and fatal sexual activity. Barton told the jury that Gladue had consented to "rough sex" with him and that the next morning, when he discovered Gladue's body, he did not seek any medical assistance and fled the scene. He later contacted police, who found Gladue's remains in a bathtub. According to the *Globe and Mail* (Carlson 2015), "Mr. Barton called police, whom he then lied to about the nature of his relationship with Ms. Gladue (his cover story was described by his lawyer as 'half-baked' and 'pathetically inept')."

At the time of her death, Gladue had a blood alcohol level four times that of the legal driving limit, which alone should have meant she could not legally consent; the Canadian Criminal Code states "there is no consent in law" when a person is "incapable of consenting to the activity" (Department of Justice 2015). Despite these facts, the all non-Indigenous jury fully acquitted Barton of all charges. On the day that protests against the decision were held in dozens of Canadian cities, the Crown announced that it would seek a retrial (Tahirali 2015).

Although white women's bodies too are subject to regulatory forces in realms including medicine, law, and violence, it is unlikely the jury would have believed that a white, non-sex-working woman had consented to the risk of death as part of a sexual encounter. We suggest that the jury was able to see kinky consensual sex as a credible explanation of Gladue's death at Barton's hands because Gladue was an Indigenous, sex-working woman. Through colonial eyes, Indigeneity and sex work are seen as so perverse as to excuse murder, whereas whiteness and the absence of sex work confer a broad range of privileges, including sexual respectability.

Ghomeshi

The second case we examine involves the use of the bogus BDSM defence at a different point in the narrative. On October 26, 2014, popular radio host Jian Ghomeshi was fired after some fourteen years with the CBC. In a public Facebook post made that evening, Ghomeshi (2014) claimed that the firing was "because of the risk of my private sex life being made public as a result of a campaign of false allegations pursued by a jilted ex-girlfriend and a freelance writer." He went on to explain that he was into BDSM, begging forgiveness if this was "shocking to some." With his post, Ghomeshi cast himself as a victim of women who felt disgusted by his kinky proclivities. At first, it seemed to be working; his Facebook post was liked thousands of times.

A *Toronto Star* article (Donovan and Brown 2014) published that same evening included allegations from three unnamed women:

> Ghomeshi physically attacked them on dates without consent. They allege he struck them with a closed fist or open hand; bit them; choked them until they almost passed out; covered their nose and mouth so that they had difficulty breathing; and that they were verbally abused during and after sex.

Ghomeshi's (2014) claims to sexual freedom ("sexual preferences are a human right") and his use of the language of consent might have exonerated him in the minds of a public just educated enough about BDSM to see it as acceptable and to stand with him against kink-shaming but not educated enough to question whether his practices truly fell within the realm of consensual, negotiated, safety-conscious BDSM. However, early public responses questioned Ghomeshi's narrative (see Zanin 2014), generating a popular conversation that began to grapple with the nature of consent in BDSM. Over the ensuing weeks, as the number of accusers grew to more than twenty (none of whom expressed disgust with BDSM), the conversation shifted away from the titillation of BDSM to focus on the pervasiveness of sexual harassment and assault in women's lives and the inadequacy of available mechanisms for recourse (see Kingston 2016). By the time Ghomeshi stood trial, the bogus BDSM defence was conspicuously absent from the narrative.

Notably, most of Ghomeshi's accusers were white women not employed in the sex industry. We posit that much of the power of the bogus BDSM defence rests on race and respectability. We can't know the rationale for Ghomeshi's change in defence tactics; however, we can note that it is much easier to project a colonial narrative about perverse sexuality onto a lone Indigenous woman in the sex industry who is not alive to speak for herself than onto non-Indigenous, non-sex-working women who are relatively privileged within the intersecting oppressive frameworks of colonialism and patriarchy. This difference, we argue, accounts at least in part for the less effective mobilization of the bogus BDSM defence in the Ghomeshi case, even though his lawyer's more classic defence approach, while widely criticized, was successful.[8]

CONCLUSION

The cases of Ghomeshi and Barton demonstrate how our cultural ambivalence about women and kinky sex plays out with vastly different consequences when we take race, sex work, and privilege into account. Nonetheless, if the Barton verdict stands, it will entrench into law the bogus BDSM defence, thus increasing the chances of its use in future cases against women at all points on the scale of privilege.

The unstable position of BDSM in the current cultural and legal imagination has contributed to mixed outcomes for the accused men in both cases. While Ghomeshi was found not guilty, he is unlikely to ever regain his status as the poster boy for progressive Canadian media. Barton's outcome remains to be seen; his lawyers have appealed to the Supreme Court of Canada to let the verdict stand and avoid a retrial (Seguin 2017), so at this time his fate remains uncertain. In short, the men's not-guilty verdicts are significant, but they do not represent clean and consequence-free conclusions to their narratives.

Mainstream society may be developing a stronger and more nuanced critical understanding of BDSM, accepting it as a valid sexuality while refusing to grant a free pass to non-consensual violence dressed up as kink. But there is much pushback against this progress and a long way to go before a robust understanding of consent, both in regard to BDSM and more broadly, is well entrenched in general practice, policy, and law.

We cannot build a critical understanding and practice of consent on the foundation of a society that systematically invalidates the consent of Indigenous women and sex workers and their right to live free from violence. Transforming consent for all women begins with protecting everyone's right to free, prior, and informed consent about decisions impacting our lives, including our political rights. This includes honouring the United Nations Declaration on the Rights of Indigenous People, signed by Canada in 2016 (Fontaine 2016). It must also include the decriminalization and destigmatization of sex work, and a stronger appreciation for sex workers' right to give and refuse consent. And, as the tide of sexual assault and harassment accusations continues to rise through movements such as #MeToo, law and policy must become more responsive and accountable to victims of sexual assault from all walks of life.

In our community and scholarly work, we are actively working toward a day when our legal systems reflect the complexities of consent in a way that recognizes individuals' agency and negotiation power while also acknowledging the ways we are all embedded in systems of power and privilege. We want to build a world where women have the right to say yes to kinky sex and no to assault — and to have both respected.

Chapter 4

A FEMINIST RESPONSE TO JUDGE LENEHAN'S RULING IN THE TRIAL OF AL-RAWI

MSVU Feminist Collective

EDITOR'S INTRODUCTION

This chapter is a feminist response to the 2017 not-guilty ruling of Judge Lenehan in the sexual assault trial of Bassam Al-Rawi in Halifax. The MSVU Feminist Collective finds Judge Lenehan's ruling in this case both incomprehensible and detrimental to the lives of young women, men, and non-binary individuals living in the region. A full transcription of the judge's decision precedes the collective's statement in the interest of allowing readers to fully apprehend its adverse impact. The transcription, reprinted below with permission, was originally published by the CBC in an article.

READ THE FULL DECISION FROM THE JUDGE
WHO SAID "CLEARLY A DRUNK CAN CONSENT":
JUDGE GREGORY LENEHAN ACQUITTED CAB
DRIVER BASSAM AL-RAWI OF SEXUAL ASSAULT

The following is the full transcript of Judge Gregory Lenehan's March 1 oral decision acquitting a Halifax taxi driver of sexually assaulting an intoxicated passenger found partly naked and unconscious in the back of his cab. The complainant's name is protected by a publication ban and any details that could identify her have been redacted. This was transcribed by CBC News based on an audio recording:

> "She doesn't recall any of that because she was drunk"
>
> Mr. Al-Rawi is before the court charged with a single count of unlawfully committing a sexual assault on (complainant) contrary to section 271 of the Criminal Code. We had a trial on this matter with a number of exhibits presented and testimony from a number of individuals.
>
> (Complainant) testified she recalled the evening of May 22, 2015, up until the time that she arrived at Boomers, a drinking establishment. She recalled consuming three drinks at that location — two tequila shots and a vodka-and-cranberry mixed drink. Her next recollection is speaking with a female police officer at some early hour of the morning of May 23, 2015, but she does not remember whether she spoke to that officer in an ambulance or in the hospital.
>
> She could not recall being prevented from re-entering Boomers after midnight on May 23, 2015, because of her level of intoxication. She does not recall her argument with her best friend and that best friend's boyfriend about going home alone in a taxi. They had tried to get a taxi for her. That exchange was somewhere between the hours of 12:15 a.m. and 12:30 a.m. on May 23, 2015. She could not recall the text exchanges that she had with two of her friends, despite the fact that she did text those individuals and carried on that communication. She does not recall hailing Mr Al-Rawi's taxi at about 1:09 a.m. and an address on Grafton

Street. And she does not recall any of those events, but all of that happened and, as I've indicated before, she actively participated in the various exchanges, the communications that were necessary in those circumstances. She doesn't recall any of that because she was drunk.

"No memory of much of what happened"

Now at about 1:20 a.m., (complainant) was found by Const. Thibault in the back seat of Mr. Al-Rawi's taxi and she was lying down with her head towards the rear passenger-side door. Her legs were up onto the seatbacks of the front bucket seats. She was naked from her breasts down. Her black wedged sandals were on the floor of the driver's compartment where Mr. Al-Rawi was located.

Her pants and underwear were in the possession of Mr. Al-Rawi as he was observed trying to shove them between the front seat and console. On the front passenger seat was (complainant)'s purse and jean jacket, her wallet and cellphone were on the floor of the front passenger compartment, as was a $20 bill. (Complainant)'s pants were actually found to be turned inside-out with the underwear caught up in the pants. And the pants were damp as a result of (complainant) having urinated while wearing her pants.

(Complainant) at 1:20 a.m. had a blood-alcohol level, which was taken back by the forensic alcohol specialist, to be equivalent of somewhere between 223 milligrams per cent and 244 milligrams per cent of alcohol. The forensic alcohol specialist (inaudible) informed that at that level of intoxication, it would appear (complainant) experienced difficulty moving, difficulty moving her perceptions and experiences from short-term memory to long-term memory. And this would explain why (complainant) was able to carry on interactions with others, but then have no memory of much of what happened from the time she arrived at Boomers and thereafter until the early hours of May 23, 2015.

Alleged victim's "DNA was in fact located above Mr. Al-Rawi's upper lip"

Other observations made of Mr. Al-Rawi at the time that Const. Thibault arrived at his vehicle. His driver's seat back was partially reclined. His pants were undone at the waist and his zipper was down a couple of inches. It was observed that the back of his pants appeared to be down about six to eight inches.

Mr. Al-Rawi was arrested by Const. Thibault. Following his arrest he was examined for possible body-substance transfer from (complainant). A DNA analysis showed (complainant)'s DNA was in fact located above Mr. Al-Rawi's upper lip. However the source, the bodily substance source, was unknown and could not be identified.

In her testimony, (complainant) said that on the date of this incident, she lived at an address on (street name) in Halifax and her usual practice when getting a taxi was to sit in the back passenger side seat, give her address to the driver, and get a $20 bill out and ready to pay for her cab ride. The presence of the $20 bill on the floor of the front passenger compartment tends to indicate that (complainant) was following her usual practice. That she was in the rear passenger-side seat also supports this indication. Her purse, jean jacket and wallet and phone in the front passenger compartment, however, is inconsistent with that. The purse and jean jacket resting on the seat cushion is also inconsistent with her having been sitting in the seat at any time prior. What do you make of it? I'm not sure.

"I have struggled to determine what all of this evidence proves"

The vehicle was examined forensically, but there was nothing presented in the Crown's case showing any of (complainant)'s bodily fluids on the fabric surfaces of the taxi. If she urinated in her pants while in the taxi, one might have expected that there would be some transfer of the fluid to the fabric of the car seats, but I had no evidence of that presented to me.

Of concern in the evidence that was presented to this court is that the taxi, 10 minutes after being hailed, was found stopped in the south end of the city, which would not be in any way in the direction one would drive for Grafton Street to get to (street name), which is just out past the Armdale Rotary.

(Complainant)'s sandals were on the floor of the driver's compartment. (Complainant)'s urine-soaked pants and panties were found turned inside-out and in the hands of Mr. Al-Rawi. Mr Al-Rawi's driver seat was partially reclined. The fact that (complainant)'s legs were resting on the top of the front — the top of the back of the front bucket seats at an angle to her torso lying on the right rear passenger seat with her head toward the door, is also of concern. So I have struggled to determine what all of this evidence proves.

"Clearly a drunk can consent"

In order for Mr. Al-Rawi to be convicted of the offence that's before the court, the Crown would have to establish beyond a reasonable doubt, that Mr. Al-Rawi touched (complainant), that it was in such a way that it violated her sexual integrity, and that it was not done with her consent. In other words, that it was done without her consent.

Now on the element of consent, in order for there to be consent, the person giving the consent must have an operating mind, they must be of an age responsible enough to agree to sexual conduct. It can be withdrawn at any time and it can be limited to certain acts and not others. A person will be incapable of giving consent if she is unconscious or is so intoxicated by alcohol or drugs as to be incapable of understanding or perceiving the situation that presents itself. This does not mean, however, that an intoxicated person cannot give consent to sexual activity. Clearly a drunk can consent.

As noted by (inaudible), the forensic alcohol specialist, one of the effects of alcohol on the human body is it tends to reduce inhibitions and increases risk-taking behaviour. And this often leads to people agreeing, and to sometimes initiating, sexual encounters, only to regret them later when they are sober.

"What is unknown"

In this case, there is no question (complainant) was drunk when she was found in Mr. Al-Rawi's taxi and she was unconscious. Therefore at that moment, when Const. Thibault approached Mr. Al-Rawi's vehicle, (complainant) was in fact incapable of consenting to any sexual activity. And that also means that whenever she did pass out, she would have been incapable.

What is unknown, however, is the moment (complainant) lost consciousness. That is important because it would appear that prior to that, she had been able to communicate with others. Although she appeared drunk to the staff at Boomers, who would not let her in because of her state of intoxication, she had appeared to make decisions for herself, however unwise those decisions might have been.

(Complainant) in her testimony could not provide any information, any details, on whether she agreed to be naked in the taxi or initiated any sexual activity. She could not provide any evidence as to why the taxi was in the south end of the city, nor could any other compellable witness provide that information.

"Crown failed to produce any evidence of lack of consent"

Now as I've said, the taxi being in the south-end neighbourhood, not on any route one would drive to get from Grafton Street to the Armdale Rotary, is of concern. (Complainant)'s sandals found on the floor of the driver's compartment under Mr. Al-Rawi's feet, is also of concern. Mr. Al-Rawi having (complainant)'s pants and panties in his hand and shoving them between the console and the front seat is of greater concern. (Complainant)'s position in the back seat with her legs propped up on the backs of the front bucket seats is very disturbing. All of that, together with (complainant) being found unconscious in the back seat of that vehicle, Mr.

Al-Rawi having his pants undone, would lead any reasonable person to believe that Mr. Al-Rawi was engaging in or about to engage in sexual activity with a woman who was incapable of consenting.

In other words, Const. Thibault had ample grounds to arrest Mr. Al-Rawi. It would have been foolish of her not to do so in the circumstances. That being said, it is the burden on the Crown to prove in this case that (complainant) could not or had not consented to any sexual activity. The Crown failed to produce any evidence of lack of consent at any time when Mr. Al-Rawi was touching (complainant).

"Only logical that those clothes came off by Mr. Al-Rawi"

I fully believe that the reason (complainant)'s sandals were in the driver's compartment is because Mr. Al-Rawi took possession of them. I also believe the pants were inside out with the panties caught up in them because Mr. Al-Rawi was the person who took them off (complainant). As described, it is only logical that those clothes came off by Mr. Al-Rawi grabbing the pants at the waist and pulling the pants and panties off together, thus turning them inside out as they were pulled over (complainant)'s legs. Anybody who has changed a child would understand the method used to strip (complainant) of her clothes.

I also believe that (complainant)'s DNA was located on Mr. Al-Rawi's upper lip because, in all probability, he wiped his hand or fingers over, either intentionally or absent-mindedly, after handling the urine-soaked pants of (complainant). That would explain her DNA being on his upper lip. So this is what I believe, and is logically probable based on the circumstantial evidence placed before me.

But I do not know whether Mr. Al-Rawi removed (complainant)'s pants at her consent, at her request, with her consent, without her consent, I don't know. The Crown marshalled no evidence on this. The Crown had no evidence to present on the issue of consent prior to Const. Thibault arriving on scene.

Taxi drivers "under a moral obligation not take advantage of intoxicated people"

Once Const. Thibault was on scene, Mr. Al-Rawi was not observed to be touching (complainant) in any way. He therefore was not assaulting her when we know she was unconscious.

Mr. Al-Rawi as a taxi driver was entrusted with the safe conduct of (complainant) to her place of residence. That is one of the main reasons we have taxis operating late at night and into the morning hours, to get people under the influence of alcohol or other intoxicants safely home.

Experienced taxi drivers easily recognize the signs of intoxication on people. They also know from experience that drunks can behave in ways detrimental to their own health and reputation. Taxi drivers are therefore under a moral obligation not take advantage of intoxicated people, either by racking up improper fares or engaging in sexual activity, as two examples.

"Not somebody I would want my daughter driving with"

If (complainant) consented to Mr. Al-Rawi's removal of her clothes, Mr. Al-Rawi was under a moral or ethical obligation to decline the invitation. She was clearly drunk. If she was unable to provide an address, he should have sought police assistance. Once he saw she had peed her pants, he knew she was quite drunk. He knew going along with any flirtation on her part involved him taking advantage of a vulnerable person. That is not somebody I would want my daughter driving with, nor any other young woman, and it is not somebody I would want to hire to drive for my company.

Having said that, with regards to the charge before this court at the critical time of when Mr. Al-Rawi would have stripped (complainant) of her clothes, the Crown has provided absolutely no evidence on the issue of lack of consent. The evidence of (inaudible) provided the possibility that with a blood-alcohol level of 223 to 244 milligrams per cent, (complainant) might very well have been capable of appearing lucid but drunk and able to direct, ask, agree or consent to any number of different activities. A lack of memory does not equate to a lack of consent. Where the Crown has failed to prove beyond a reasonable doubt (complainant)'s lack of consent, I am left with no alternative but to find Mr. Al-Rawi not guilty.

Mr. Al-Rawi, you're free to go. Thank you.

THE MSVU FEMINIST COLLECTIVE'S RESPONSE TO JUDGE LENEHAN'S RULING

In the wake of the Judge Lehenan's not-guilty ruling in the sexual assault trial of cab driver Bassam Al-Rawi, many young women and non-binary individuals in Halifax were left feeling helpless. This feeling arises very logically. In light of the facts of the case, which were affirmed by the judge, the young woman's incapacity to consent should have been obvious, yet, incomprehensible to us, Lenehan found that the Crown had proven neither lack of consent nor incapacity to consent.

In a world where we are constantly reminded of our own vulnerability to intimate partner violence or sexual violence, we are forced to navigate our lives in fear and distrust. We learn that we must take certain precautions and place restrictions on our freedom to avoid violence. We learn that if we are sexually assaulted, others will find ways to blame us for the violation of our bodies and autonomy. Once again, Lenehan's ruling shows us how deeply victim blaming is entrenched in the criminal justice system, which consistently fails to support victims of sexual violence or to hold perpetrators accountable.

Women who testify against their rapists in court are routinely humiliated, degraded, and retraumatized. Their credibility is questioned, and every aspect of their behaviour is scrutinized, often through a gender-biased and misogynistic lens. How high is the bar for victims to be believed? In this case, a young woman was found by a police officer, unconscious and half-naked in the backseat of a cab, while the cab driver tried to hide her urine-soaked pants and underwear. Judge Lenehan "struggled" — as he explained in his ruling — to determine the meaning of that evidence. It was still possible, he thought, that the woman had consented. Despite the fact that when the police officer arrived at the vehicle, Al-Rawi was parked in a location far from the young woman's home or the place she was picked up, with his pants unzipped and the woman's DNA on his mouth, he was found not guilty of sexual assault.

The community responded with outrage and demands for systemic change. The MSVU Feminist Collective, as a student society dedicated to providing Mount Saint Vincent University students with a platform for discussion, education, and activism on feminist issues, joined others in the community at a rally calling for the removal of Judge Lenehan from the bench. Even those familiar with the despairingly low conviction rates for sexual assault were surprised that a judge could be faced with so much circumstantial evidence without finding the Crown had made its case. Judge Lenehan's statement that "clearly, a drunk can consent" and his suggestion that the woman might have consented prior to losing consciousness were deemed insensitive, irresponsible, and inaccurate by many who claimed that he had failed to uphold the laws around consent.

How could proper consent be obtained from a woman who was so intoxicated that she was prevented from entering a bar, lost control of her bladder, lost consciousness, and could not remember any details of being in the cab? How could a cab driver, someone in a position of trust who was responsible for getting passengers home safely, not be held account-able for taking advantage of an intoxicated woman? And what options are women and non-binary individuals left with when the systems they are told to rely on for support, safety, protection, and justice fail to do so at every turn?

Judge Lenehan's ruling reveals once again that rape myths, stereotypes, and ideas about women's sexuality shape how Canadian law handles issues of consent. He found that Al-Rawi — who was a complete stranger to the woman in his cab — was likely responsible for removing her cloth-ing and that sexual activity had taken place. Furthermore, the judge was clear that Al-Rawi was under an ethical obligation to refuse any sexual advances from an intoxicated passenger. Yet the judge refused to find any legal wrongdoing.

What does this legal decision teach other men who view women as sexual objects and feel entitled to women's bodies? For some, it will con-firm pornographic male fantasies, which played out during this case, of sexually available and promiscuous young women willing to have sex with anyone at any time and always "asking for it." Others will be reassured that a woman's lack of consent need not stand as a barrier to sexually using her body.

As young women, men, and non-binary individuals, we are greatly concerned with the implications of this ruling. We are concerned with the dangerous ideas about consent that it perpetuates, as well as the role of the legal system in contributing to a wider culture that normalizes, trivializes, and accepts sexual violence. This ruling shows the need for legal clarification around sexual consent, specialized training for judges handling sexual assault cases, and alternative options for safe transportation. It also reveals the need for cultural changes in the way we understand sexual violence and consent to ensure that gender biases and rape myths are kept out of the courtroom.

|

Chapter 5

THE BLUNT INSTRUMENT
OF THE LAW

Consent and HIV Non-Disclosure

San Patten and Alison Symington

HIV is known as the most stigmatized modern illness, due to its association with marginalized and often criminalized populations and practices. HIV-related stigma and discrimination are barriers to HIV information, prevention, care, and treatment. They also discourage people living with HIV from disclosing their status to sexual partners and others (UNAIDS 2014). One of the most insidious manifestations of HIV stigma in contemporary Canadian society is the criminalization of HIV non-disclosure. With over 200 prosecutions as of 2017, Canada has the third-largest absolute number of prosecutions for HIV non-disclosure in the world, and one of the highest per capita rates of prosecution given the number of people living with HIV in the country (Hastings, Kazatchkine, and Mykhalovskiy 2016). Furthermore, Canada is exceptional in that it treats HIV non-disclosure as a sexual offence and a crime of *risk* of bodily harm as opposed to requiring actual harm (Canadian HIV/AIDS Legal Network 2014).

Does failing to reveal one's HIV-positive status before sex merit criminalization? Does non-disclosure violate the autonomy and dignity of the sexual partner such that it should be prosecuted as sexual assault? Canadian law says "yes" when the possibility of transmission is deemed "realistic." This chapter argues that, rather than protecting sexual autonomy and dignity, criminalizing HIV does injustice to many individuals charged. Moreover, it further compromises the capacity of our criminal justice system, which has never effectively stemmed sexual assault, to respond to sexual violence. We therefore advocate for a law reform approach that removes HIV non-disclosure cases from the sphere of consent and sexual assault. Composed in a Q&A style, this chapter explores issues of consent in relation to HIV non-disclosure and the unusual application of sexual assault law to HIV non-disclosure cases.

WHAT IS THE CURRENT STATE OF THE LAW?

Canada's bespoke legal approach to HIV was established by the 1998 Supreme Court of Canada (SCC) decision in the *Cuerrier* case, which involved a man who had condomless sex with two women without first disclosing his HIV-positive status. The court ruled in this case that when there is a "significant risk of serious bodily harm," not disclosing amounts to a "fraud"[1] that invalidates the partner's consent to sex, rendering the sexual encounter an assault (Elliott 1999). The Court ruled that when one partner is HIV-positive, penile-vaginal sex without a condom constitutes significant risk, and HIV infection constitutes serious bodily harm. At the time of the ruling, HIV treatment was only newly available, and knowledge about treatment effectiveness and consequent transmission risk was rudimentary. HIV infection was seen as inevitably leading to AIDS, an incurable and fatal illness. Based on this understanding of HIV, the SCC established that non-disclosure could result in charges of aggravated assault or aggravated sexual assault (Symington 2009).

In 2012, the SCC revisited this issue, reaffirming that there is a duty to disclose if there is a "significant risk of serious bodily harm." It also decided that "significant risk" for cases involving HIV meant "realistic possibility of HIV transmission" (*R. v. Mabior*, 2012 SCC 47; *R. v. D.C.*, 2012 SCC 48). From this point forward, before having sex that poses "a realistic possibility of transmission," a person living with HIV is legally required to disclose to their partner. According to the new doctrine of "realistic possibility," condom use does not alleviate the obligation to disclose. The SCC also examined the issue of viral load. As discussed in the following section, modern HIV treatment can reduce viral load to an undetectable level, at which point transmission no longer occurs. Nonetheless, the court suggested that having a low or undetectable viral load may not on its own (i.e., without condom use) reduce the possibility of transmission sufficiently to remove the disclosure obligation.

In summary, as a result of 2012 SCC decisions, to secure a sexual assault conviction for HIV non-disclosure, the prosecution must prove beyond a reasonable doubt the following:

1. the HIV-positive partner (who knows their status) did not disclose this to their sexual partner (or they actively deceived their partner);
2. in the circumstances of the sexual encounter, there was a "realistic possibility of transmitting HIV" to the sexual partner; and
3. the partner would not have consented to the sexual encounter had they known the other person to be HIV-positive.

If the prosecution proves these things, they have established that the accused person living with HIV obtained their partner's consent to sex by "fraud." Therefore, their partner's consent to sex was not legally valid and they have committed a sexual assault (*Mabior* and *DC*, SCC 2012).

WHAT DO WE KNOW ABOUT HIV AND ITS TRANSMISSION?

Medical science is key to these criminal cases, as risk level is the defining element in determining whether HIV disclosure is legally required. There have been dramatic (and wonderful) changes in HIV science in the last twenty years. The following is now clearly established, as verified by large international studies (Cohen et al. 2016; Eshleman et al. 2017; Supervie et al. 2014) and as articulated in a strong consensus statement by nearly eighty leading Canadian HIV researchers and clinicians in 2014 and reiterated in early 2017 (Loutfy et al. 2014; Loutfy et al. 2017):

1. An unbroken condom, used correctly, is 100 percent effective at stopping HIV transmission.
2. With access to treatment, HIV is a chronic manageable illness.

Treatment not only allows people to live long and healthy lives but also prevents HIV transmission to sexual partners by reducing a person's viral load.

3. Vaginal or anal sex without a condom poses no risk of transmission when the HIV-positive partner is on effective antiretroviral therapy.

The real game changer in HIV prevention science is that an individual who has an undetectable viral load cannot transmit HIV. The legal tests are based on an understanding of HIV as easily transmissible and necessarily fatal. This logic simply does not hold true now that we live in what a global prevention campaign has dubbed the "U=U" era, meaning "Undetectable=Untransmittable" (Prevention Access Campaign 2016).

HOW DID HIV NON-DISCLOSURE BECOME CONCEPTUALIZED AS (AGGRAVATED) SEXUAL ASSAULT?

Because the courts still consider HIV infection to "endanger life," when people are charged for failure to disclose, they are usually charged with aggravated sexual assault. This is the most serious form of sexual assault in the Criminal Code and a charge seldom used in other sexual assault cases. Aggravated sexual assault usually involves extreme violence, brutality, and grievous injury. A conviction carries a maximum penalty of life imprisonment and mandatory registration as a sexual offender.

To understand the origins of this approach, it is helpful to recall one of Canada's earliest and most notorious HIV prosecutions: the case of Charles Ssenyonga. An immigrant from Uganda, Ssenyonga was living in London, Ontario, in 1989 when he was issued an order by the public health authorities to cease sexual contact. He had been identified as the origin of two women's HIV infections, which makes this case unusual in that most criminal cases (including the *Cuerrier* case) do not involve transmission. Ssenyonga refused to comply, and in 1991 four charges were brought against him: aggravated sexual assault, criminal negligence causing bodily harm, criminal negligence unlawfully causing bodily harm, and committing a common nuisance (Miller 2005). As the case proceeded, only the charge of sexual assault stuck. His case fed into the "Western fantasy of containing AIDS in Africa" (Miller 2005) and resonated with the racist stereotype that Black men take advantage of white women, which legal historians have identified as prominent in early Canadian law:

> Black men and women were presumed to possess a pathological sexuality that threatened to contaminate Canada's white settlers. The Black male-as-rapist trope proved quite powerful in Canada, and the anti-Black hysteria linking Blackness to sexual danger that permeated the media and public opinion had a foothold within the highest levels of government. (Maynard 2017: 41).

Ssenyonga evoked outrage among some prominent feminists, including June Callwood and Michele Landsberg, and triggered a feminist rally for HIV criminalization in Canada that framed non-disclosure as an affront to dignity and autonomy and as a new form of violence against women. Addressing HIV non-disclosure as sexual assault rather than as a public health matter was understood as a feminist intervention to protect women. This rationale was put before the courts by the Manitoba Attorney General in the ground-breaking *Mabior* case (2010). Relying on the leading sexual assault cases of *Ewanchuk* and *J.A.,* the Attorney General wrote:

> Having control over who touches one's body, and how, lies at the core of human dignity and autonomy.... Denying a complainant the ability to decide for herself whether — and, if so, how — she is willing to subject herself to the risk of HIV infection goes against everything this fundamental right stands for. No one else is entitled to make this decision for her. The fact that an accused uses condoms or takes medication to reduce his risk of infection does not change the basic truth: despite our best medical efforts to date, sexual intercourse with an HIV-positive individual continues to carry the chance that the virus will be transmitted. If transmission occurs, the consequences for the complainant are permanent, incurable, life-altering and potentially fatal. (AG Manitoba SCC Factum, Mabior. Citations omitted).

Similarly, Carissima Mathen and Michael Plaxton (2011) argued that by not disclosing, a person living with HIV objectifies their sexual partner and denies their autonomy:

> A partner's failure to ask about matters of sexual health provides a poor basis for inferring indifference to it … to automatically proceed on the basis that one's partner is not invested in her own health and well-being, and is therefore willing to make herself sexually available in spite of obvious risks — may be to treat her as if she had no plans or priorities beyond her own immediate sexual gratification. It effectively denies that one's partner has any *meaningful* autonomy in *any* sphere, not just in the immediate sexual context.

Denial of autonomy is thus placed as the key rationale for criminalizing HIV non-disclosure as sexual assault. In what follows, we argue that achieving autonomy through full information is an impracticable objective and moreover that mandating disclosure only of HIV-positive status amounts to perpetuation of discrimination and stigma.

CAN A PERSON CONSENT TO SEX WITHOUT KNOWING THAT THE PARTNER IS LIVING WITH HIV?

In medicine, the standard of practice is informed consent, documented in writing prior to the procedure or study, after informing the patient of possible risks and complications. In signing a contract or engaging in financial transactions, there must be disclosures about risks and conditions. Of course, "affirmative consent" rather than "informed consent" is the standard for consent to sex under Canadian law. Most sexual assault cases revolve around determining if a person has forced or coerced someone to have sex against their will. The SCC established the disclosure standard for HIV based on the idea that HIV status was necessary information for consent. Upon disclosing their HIV-positive status, however, people living with HIV are often compelled to become educators, explaining the science of HIV transmission and risk. Full information requires not only disclosure but a fulsome discussion about treatment, viral load, and chances of transmission, which as we have noted become negligible with effective treatment.

One wonders why HIV status should be singled out by the courts. What else is necessary information in order to consent to sex? Should an individual be charged with sexual assault if they don't disclose that their current gender doesn't match the sex they were assigned at birth? What about reproductive intentions, marital status, religion, or wealth? What about a history of committing gender-based violence? Sexual assault convictions on the grounds of fraud provoke questions about whether courts can formulate a reasonable test for sexual fraud when sex happens in so many different relational contexts. In fact, outside of HIV non-disclosure cases, the sexual fraud provisions of the law have not seen much action since *Cuerrier*. Attempts to use the fraud-vitiating-consent doctrine to charge a client who refused to pay a sex worker have failed.[2] A civil action seeking damages for the emotional harm resulting from unplanned parenthood also failed.[3] Paradoxically, now that having sex with someone who is living with HIV does not have "lethal consequences" (*R. v. Cuerrier* 1998), the law is becoming more aggressive — both in terms of enforcement and doctrine. Given advancements in HIV treatment, defining positive status as information that must be disclosed for consent to be considered valid boils down to stigma and discrimination.

DOESN'T CRIMINALIZATION OF HIV NON-DISCLOSURE PROTECT WOMEN?

In both 1998 and 2012, one of the underlying justifications for the SCC's rulings was to protect women. However, although the majority of those charged and convicted have been men who have not disclosed to their female sexual partners, criminalizing HIV non-disclosure as a form of sexual assault does little to protect women. This is true for three reasons.

First, HIV epidemics are driven by undiagnosed HIV infections, not by people who know their HIV-positive status. Given that approximately 20 percent of HIV infections in Canada are undiagnosed (Public Health Agency of Canada 2017), relying on disclosure rather than safer sex practices for HIV prevention creates a false sense of security and increases risk of infection from people living with undiagnosed HIV. Furthermore, such an approach undermines the message that it is the responsibility of all sexually active persons to practise safer sex and leads to a false sense of security that no such measures are necessary in the absence of disclosure by a sexual partner.

Second, criminalizing HIV non-disclosure as sexual assault may make it more difficult to prosecute cases of sexual assault in the traditional sense of gender-based violence. Though a minuscule percentage of the sexual assault cases that are brought to police and prosecutors, HIV non-disclosure cases are shaping sexual assault law. We have seen this in the case of *R. v. Hutchison,* which dealt with a deception regarding contraception, not HIV. The SCC used the fraud interpretation from its earlier HIV decisions, excising *how* the sexual touching takes place — a key consideration according to the same court's reasoning in *Ewanchuk* — from the preliminary question of consent. *Hutchinson* looks at the issue of consent to sex without considering violence or equality. Arguably, *Hutchinson* has left us with weaker protection of sexual autonomy and integrity, which could make it more difficult for survivors of sexual assault to establish their cases going forward.

Central to efforts of legal feminists to improve sexual assault law has been the push for a robust definition of consent. When police, prosecutors, and judges apply the law of sexual assault to HIV non-disclosure cases, which are quite distinct from other sorts of sexual assault, the law could be distorted. While the criminal law on sexual assault has been largely ineffective in terms of bringing justice to survivors or quelling the assaultive behaviour in our society, it nonetheless can be an important tool to advance gender equality by setting normative standards with respect to sexual behaviour (Canadian HIV/AIDS Legal Network 2014; Canadian HIV/AIDS Legal Network and Goldelox Productions 2015.).

The third reason that criminalization of HIV non-disclosure as sexual assault does little to protect women relates to power. Perpetrators of sexual assault exercise power over another person, disrespecting that person's autonomy and dignity through objectification, forcing or coercing sex, or both. However, the actions and relationships engaged in HIV non-disclosure cases do not conform to this picture. Rather, in a development that was seemingly unanticipated by the SCC and early supporters of HIV criminalization, the law is being used to abuse and control vulnerable women and youth — a fact that raises serious questions about whether sexual assault law is indeed an appropriate mechanism to redress HIV non-disclosure. Consider the following stories of women who have been convicted for HIV non-disclosure in Canada.

Diane, a French-Canadian woman living near Montreal, began dating a man she met at her son's soccer game. He found out that she was living with HIV and broke up with her, but then they got back together and lived together for several years. He became violent towards her. In a final altercation at her house, Diane's son tried to defend her, and the man broke her son's hand and badly beat her. He was convicted for this abuse but given an absolute discharge at sentencing when he falsely alleged that he and Diane had unprotected sex and she had not disclosed her HIV status. At trial, she was convicted (later overturned on appeal).

Marjory is an Indigenous woman living with HIV in Manitoba with a history of sexual and physical abuse, drug addiction and alcoholism, and poverty. She was convicted for HIV non-disclosure in relation to three sexual encounters with a "friend." She was intoxicated each time. The man initiated the sex each time, and she didn't resist. He later found out that she was living with HIV, and she was charged and convicted of aggravated sexual assault.[4]

May was a sex worker in Thailand who immigrated to Canada. She had tested positive for HIV before immigrating, but during her immigration medical examination, no one mentioned HIV so she assumed the previous test results were incorrect. She had a very low level of literacy and spoke little English. Her Canadian husband became infected. She was charged, convicted, and ultimately deported back to Thailand.

Twenty of the approximately 200 known charges for HIV non-disclosure have been filed against women, and few of these cases have involved HIV transmission (Hastings et al. 2016). The cruel irony of women being charged with sexual assault for HIV non-disclosure is that many of the women charged are themselves survivors of sexual violence. Neuroscience has shown that effects of childhood sexual and physical abuse may contribute to adulthood psychopathological conditions (Heim et al. 2000), including the inability to communicate and respond normally when triggered, which in turn may hinder disclosure. Is it conscionable to prosecute a woman living with HIV who is a survivor of violence and abuse, in circumstances where she may be unable to disclose as a result of natural neurobiological reactions to the trauma she has experienced?

Disclosing HIV to a partner can be met with violence, rejection, and abandonment, particularly for women living in abusive situations, and the very act of disclosing creates vulnerability to false accusations, coercion, and even violence (Allard, Kazatchkine, and Symington 2013). Furthermore, women convicted of aggravated sexual assault will be registered as sex offenders; likely those who assaulted them are not on the registry.

CONCLUSION

In dealing with HIV non-disclosure cases, one approach would be continuing to employ the current fraud provisions in the law while accepting that there is no realistic possibility of transmission, and therefore no obligation to disclose, when a person living with HIV is receiving effective treatment, using condoms, or both. We, however, would prefer an approach that takes as its starting point the delinking of HIV disclosure from issues of consent and sexual assault. We acknowledge that not disclosing HIV-positive status can be a means to objectify, exploit, and/or abuse a sexual partner. But when it is such, the non-disclosure is seldom the only behaviour in the relationship that is objectifying, exploitative, or abusive. By isolating the non-disclosure for aggressive legal punishment, the law ignores the medical science of HIV transmission and misnames the abuse for some while unjustly prosecuting others. People will be most effectively empowered to negotiate sex not through criminalization that results from and reinforces the very stigma that makes disclosure both difficult and dangerous, but in safe and inclusive social environments that support their health and dignity.

Chapter 6

THE ILLUSION OF INCLUSION IN YORK UNIVERSITY'S SEXUAL ASSAULT POLICYMAKING PROCESS

Mandi Gray, Laura Pin, and Annelies Cooper

In 2016, the Ontario government passed Bill 132, Sexual Violence and Harassment Action Plan Act (Supporting Survivors, Challenging Sexual Violence and Harassment). It states that all post-secondary institutions receiving public funds must have developed and implemented a stand-alone sexual assault policy by January 1, 2017. It also requires that university administrators consider "student input" during the development of the policy and that they review the policy every three years thereafter (Legislative Assembly of Ontario 2016).

In this chapter we examine the role of student consultation and involvement in the development of York University's stand-alone sexual assault policy. Drawing on our experiences as participants in the policy development process, we argue that meaningful student consultation was both illusory and strategically mobilized to legitimate the exclusion of sexual violence experts. We argue that within neoliberalized institutions, consultation is often used along with discursive markers such as "engagement" and "collaboration" to appease stakeholders without substantively addressing their concerns. In the case of York's redevelopment of its sexual assault policy, student consultation was carried out to legitimate rather than shape a sexual assault policy that in fact had been produced in advance. The policy was then branded "student-led" even as the voices of anti-violence activists, feminist scholars specialized in sexual violence, and those directly affected by sexual assault on campus were sidelined.

SILENCE IS VIOLENCE

The authors of this chapter are members of a student activist group called Silence is Violence (SiV), which started at York University in March 2015, the year preceding passage of Bill 132. The group initially met after doctoral student Mandi Gray was sexually assaulted by another PhD student in early 2015.[1] In the same month the assault was reported, York University implemented its Policy on Sexual Assault Awareness, Prevention and Response. On paper, the policy appeared progressive, explicitly defining consent and rape culture and also using the language of "survivor-centric" to describe its approach to sexual assault (the policy has since been changed and no longer includes this term). In practice, the policy had several gaps, including a failure to outline institutional procedures for disclosures or reports of sexual assault. In the absence of such procedures, survivors may be compelled to tell their stories repeatedly or to disclose to parties whose responses may be shaped by rape mythology. Depending on the staff person taking the disclosure or formal report, the survivors' experiences are often minimized or dismissed altogether. Survivors' reports may result in no response whatsoever or require the survivor to report to the police in order to invoke a university response. In response, SiV started organizing to raise awareness about York's lack of institutional procedures for responding to a report of sexual assault and York's wholly inadequate support services and academic and workplace accommodations for those impacted by campus sexual assault.

"CONSULTATION" AND THE NEOLIBERAL UNIVERSITY

After Bill 132 was passed, York University revised its existing Policy on Sexual Assault Awareness, Prevention and Response with interim measures while developing a new policy that would adhere to the legislative requirement that policy development include processes for "consider[ing] student input" (Legislative Assembly of Ontario 2016). Specifically,

York set up a number of consultations in the fall of 2016. The university reported that thirty-five consultations, three of which were open to the York community at large, took place with a total of six hundred students, faculty, and staff (York University n.d.). In addition, the university circulated a survey for feedback on the interim sexual violence policy and received forty responses (York University n.d.). On December 14, 2016, the York University Board of Governors approved the new Policy on Sexual Violence (York University Secretariat Policies 2016). This rapid turnaround is among a number of elements of the policy development timeline that lead us to question the integrity of the consultation process.

As York rolled out its new Policy on Sexual Violence, its public relations efforts were focused on the consultation process (York University 2016, n.d.). The rhetoric of consultation served several purposes for the university: It met the legislative obligations of Bill 132, it legitimized the new policy, and it fortified York's corporate brand as a post-secondary institution committed to social justice and progressive politics. This commitment is articulated in the university's mission statement, which envisions York as a "community of faculty, students, staff, alumni and volunteers committed to academic freedom, social justice, accessible education, and collegial self-governance" (Gray and Pin 2017; York University n.d.). Announcing the approval of the new sexual violence policy, York issued a press release that said the following:

> The policy confirms the University's longstanding commitment to foster a culture where attitudes and behaviors that perpetuate sexual violence are rejected, survivors are supported, and those who are found to have committed sexual violence are held accountable.

In the press release, York University utilizes feminist rhetoric and references the importance of recognizing the "intersectional experiences of survivors and the barriers that they face." It proclaims its determination "to break down those barriers wherever possible" by "providing survivor-centric supports and services" on campus (York University 2016).

We suggest that York's rhetoric of representative consultation together with its dismissal of sexual assault survivors and experts belonging to its campus community forms a contradiction that is consistent with neoliberalism. Neoliberalism involves directing state expenditures away from publicly funded programs in areas ranging from health care to post-secondary education. Cuts are legitimized by an ideology that emphasizes an individual's responsibility for their own well-being or lack thereof. As neoliberalism has gained steam, North American post-secondary institutions, including York University, have undergone restructuring in response to declines in the proportion of operating revenue derived from government funding. Student tuition fees now make up 50 percent of York University's operating revenue (Lebane and Cherry 2016). The resulting dependence on enrolment makes student recruitment, and consequently branding, essential to the university's operating budget.

Following numerous high-profile incidents at York University, including seventeen sexual assaults in 2012, York received an influx of negative media attention questioning campus safety. For example, a *Toronto Life* article characterized York as a "hunting ground for sexual predators" (Laidlaw 2013: 68). The university did not respond by directing funds to addressing the structural and institutional barriers faced by community members who experience sexual violence on campus. Instead, it committed funds to three other areas, none of which, from our perspective, served survivors.

First, in an initiative that made no attempt to address the problem of sexual assault on campus, the university invested in a multi-million-dollar publicity campaign titled "this is my time" in an effort to redefine the tarnished reputation of the school after a flurry of negative publicity related to labour disruptions and on-campus safety issues (CASSIES n.d.; York University 2014). The campaign featured York students sharing aspirational visions of their contributions to the world in a future year. The aim was to "own the future" by sending the message to prospective students that York "will give [them] both the excellent academic foundation and the real world experiences [they] need to channel [their] passions into actions" (CASSIES n.d). The campaign is credited for successfully reversing some of York's decline in student applications (Glovasky 2014; York University 2014).

Second, York University invested in significant security upgrades on campus. It had a safety audit conducted by a not-for-profit anti-violence organization, expanded its security staff, created a smartphone app for instant security notifications, and installed additional closed-circuit television video surveillance on campus (Gregory 2012; Gray and Pin 2017). As a response to sexual violence, securitization holds great appeal for the neoliberalized university: It is relatively easy to enact, highly visible, and responsive to student myths concerning the location and nature of sexual assault. However, critical feminist scholars argue that securitization discourses capitalize upon women's fear of crime "by commodifying safety in the form of gadgets, alarms, and workshops that socialize women to be ever more fearful" (Hall 2004: 4). Unfortunately, security responses to sexual assault are more beneficial to university branding than they are to university community members who experience sexual violence as a result of larger structural changes (Gray and Pin 2017; Gregory 2012).

Third, York put money into a campaign titled "Safer Together," presenting campus safety from assault in terms of individualized risk management by prospective victims, reminding members of the university community to "do their part" to ensure their own safety and the safety of others through personal vigilance (Gray and Pin 2017). This rhetoric shifts responsibility for campus safety risks onto individualized subjects, reflecting discourses of responsibilization and individualization that rationalize neoliberal ideologies and techniques of governance (Brown 2015).

ADMINISTRATIVE DOMINANCE AND THE ILLUSION OF INCLUSION

The Canadian Federation of Students, Canada's largest post-secondary student lobbying group, successfully advocated for student consultation as a mandatory step in developing campus sexual assault policies under Bill 132. SiV supports the involvement of students in the development of these policies for two closely knit reasons. First, we favour redressing the democratic deficit inherent in a university structure that denies power to the very students who endure many of the negative consequences of neoliberal restructuring. Second, we adhere to the democratic principle that those affected by a decision should help to make it. Following from our democratic values, we have two interrelated concerns with the consultation process that unfolded at York. We argue that surface-level student and community consultation has been used to mask administrative dominance in the policymaking process. Further, we argue that student and community inclusion were used to legitimate exclusion of expert and first-hand knowledge about sexual assault and sexual violence.

York's representation of the sexual assault policy as predominantly driven by students and community obscures the top-down nature of the policymaking process. The university's communications about the consultation process represented the working group as "widely representative of the community" (Castle 2016). However, in meetings with a number of working group appointees, SiV found that the group consisted mainly of administrators and staff with a handful of hand-picked student representatives and a single faculty member. In the absence of any university-wide process to solicit student involvement, the administration invited particular students to participate. Moreover, some student groups were unaware that York University had advertised their participation in the working group, as they had not been invited to any meetings. The sole faculty member on the working group had no research experience or publications in the area of sexual violence. Within a couple months, the faculty member resigned her position in the working group and it was left unfilled, despite the presence on York campus of many academics with expertise in sexual and gender-based violence.

Despite the representation of the sexual violence policy working group as open to student input, SiV was repeatedly denied a seat and had to struggle for the opportunity to merely present our recommendations. After increasing advocacy efforts, including contacting the media, SiV was finally invited to attend a working group meeting to present our recommendations, which included the following:

- a fully funded centralized feminist support service for survivors of violence,
- appointment of a member of SiV to the working group,
- discontinuation of the use of the Office of Student Community Relations to handle reports of sexual violence (due to its lack of expertise in the area of sexual violence and its reliance on an adversarial tribunal to process complaints that included cross-examination of survivors by their perpetrators),

- consultation with external feminist legal counsel with expertise advocating for survivors of sexual violence,
- active and ongoing inclusion of campus sexual assault survivors, and
- consultation of survivors in campus safety planning to be conducted with woman-identified and LGBTQ staff members familiar with interpersonal and sexual violence. (Silence is Violence 2016)

Many of our concerns pertained to the availability of campus resources and the institutional responses to reports of sexual assault. The official minutes from that meeting label our concerns "misinformation" and also state that working group members were concerned "that communication from Silence is Violence may discourage other survivors from accessing service on campus ... [and that SiV's work was] undoing trust that has been built because damage [was] being done at the grassroots level" (Sexual Assault Awareness, Prevention, and Response Policy Working Group Meeting Notes 2015). On the contrary, it is our position that any student mistrust of York's responses to sexual assault was created by York's responses to sexual assault, not by student activism drawing attention to gaps in those responses, and notably not by activism of student survivors who have direct experience with York's responses to sexual violence. Following that meeting, our request to have a seat on the working group was once again denied.

Furthermore, although the "consultation period" was stated to have commenced in October, working group members were required to keep policy drafts confidential until late November and were unable to comment on the specifics of the draft during the consultation period. As concerned members of the York community, we found it very frustrating to consult on something we could not assess. Three publicly open consultations occurred, but they were held within three weeks of the final approval of the policy and were announced with only two to five days' notice, suggesting a lack of genuine interest in gathering the perspectives of York community members.

SiV has not been alone in experiencing an adversarial relationship with the working group. CUPE 3903, the union representing York University contract faculty, teaching assistants, and graduate assistants, was shut out of the group until September 30, 2016. Once at the working group table, CUPE representatives found that the policy draft was near completion, that longstanding issues raised by the union and SiV had been largely unaddressed, and input from union members remained unwelcome. On November 24, 2016, CUPE 3903 released a statement publicly withdrawing from the working group due to process-related dissatisfaction. Specifically, the statement raised concerns about the lack of "substantial consultation," with the only open consultations occurring just weeks before the official policy would be passed through the York University Board of Governors in December 2016. The CUPE 3903 Trans Feminist Action Caucus (2016) stated that "nothing in the process indicates that survivors have been actively engaged" in the consultation and that York University uses the language of "survivor-centric" but "this has been merely a rhetorical device." The draft policy was not made public to the university community until December 5, 2016, nine days before the Board of Governors would meet to vote on the policy (York University 2016). Students at large were never afforded an opportunity to address the Board of Governors concerning the policy. Thus, the actual decision-making process was insulated from the student and community consultations. It is unclear if or how results of the consultations were integrated into the policy at all.

Even were it the case that student and community input had been integrated into the sexual assault policy, it seems that input from those best positioned to guide sexual assault policy development would not have led the process. York's sexual assault policy is described as "stemming from our community consultations," with "over 60 hours of consultation" to be precise (York University 2016). Students are listed first among community members consulted and a number of student groups are represented in the working group, yet there is no record of consultation with survivor-led groups or sexual violence experts. York University is home to feminist researchers, including legal scholars with years of experience researching sexual violence. Exclusion of these researchers suggests that the corporate university does not value the expertise that makes up the academy.

As mentioned earlier, York University, like post-secondary institutions broadly across North America, has undergone restructuring under neoliberal pressures of austerity and public funding cuts to mimic corporate structures. Neoliberal restructuring impacts sexual assault policy formation in two ways. First, university branding and public relations acquire new importance to maintain student recruitment and increase enrolment. Because student tuition fees make up half of York University's revenue, the maintenance of student enrolment is crucial for its operating budget (Lebane and Cherry 2016). This dependence on student enrolments has placed a newfound emphasis on the public image of the university and explains why York's response to falling enrolments and a degradation of reputation — in part related to campus safety — was a multi-million-dollar media campaign. While the campaign was incredibly successful in reversing some of York's decline in student applications, there was not an accompanying or equivalent expenditure on student services and supports in the face of campus safety concerns. What this has amounted to in the latest iteration of York's public image crafting in terms of policy formation has been an increase in the formal appearance of student involvement. In this context of neoliberal austerity and entrepreneurialism, student consultations are operationalized towards York's public image of progressiveness and inclusivity, and commodified to entice and retain the monetary investment of the student (consumer) in the form of tuition dollars.

CONCLUSION

In sum, York curated student participation to give the appearance of representing and responding to student stakeholders, while faculty sexual violence experts were sidelined and student advocates who were open about their experiential knowledge of sexual violence and of institutional responses to sexual violence were treated as disruptive agitators. This set of strategies enabled and legitimated adoption of an administratively driven sexual assault policy. Clearer language in Bill 132 that goes beyond "consider[ing] student input" to specify how consultation results must be incorporated into policy would help drive more substantial engagement with students. But student consultation is insufficient to create a policy that supports people who have experienced sexual violence. Sexual assault policymaking should be actively directed by people who have knowledge of the dynamics of sexual violence. This would require a shift in university governance that is unlikely to occur given the neoliberal context of declining public funding and increased competition. This context leaves university administrations more reluctant than ever to take actions that might reveal institutional shortcomings like alarming rates of sexual assault on campus. Yet meaningfully addressing sexual violence requires visibility of the problem, conflict over solutions, and the adoption of practices that may contravene neoliberal logics. In an era of fiscal austerity, it would require universities to spend money on student supports; at a time of sleek advertising campaigns, it would require openness about the widespread incidence of sexual violence; and in a place where consultation is about producing agreement, it would require the facilitation of spaces open to dissenting views.

Chapter 7

MILITARY SEXUAL VIOLENCE IN CANADA

Maya Eichler

Feminist scholars and activists have documented the close ties between militarization and sexual violence across history and geography (Enloe 2000; Goldstein 2001). War and military conflict include the systematic use of rape as a weapon. The deployment of military troops is known to increase the risk of sexual exploitation and abuse of girls and women in conflict zones. Militarization exacerbates gender inequalities and gender-based violence in a myriad of ways. This chapter focuses on another aspect of sexual violence linked to military power — namely, the sexual violence perpetrated within militaries towards military personnel.

Military sexual violence is a global problem, and Canada is no exception. In 2016, a Statistics Canada survey found that four in five military members reported "seeing, hearing or experiencing inappropriate sexual or discriminatory behaviour" in their workplace. It also found that women in the Canadian military experienced sexual assault[1] at higher rates than did military men, and both women and men in the military experienced higher rates of sexual assault than civilians. In Canada, close to one in three women are sexually assaulted during their military career, in contrast to 4 percent of men (Cotter 2016).

What explains these stunning rates of sexual violence in the Canadian military? How has the military responded? And what is needed to bring about change? Root causes of sexual violence such as gender stereotypes, histories of gender discrimination, codes of silence, and inadequate legal recourse exist across the military and civilian spheres. Military sexual violence is connected to sexual violence in societies at large. However, militaries have specific characteristics that make the problem of military sexual violence particularly intractable.

In this chapter, I argue that sexual violence is not a coincidental part of military life. It is linked to key features of the military's history, culture, and organization. A legacy of women's marginalization within the Canadian Armed Forces (CAF) and a gendered culture that celebrates masculinity and denigrates femininity place women in marginal, subordinate, and therefore vulnerable positions. In addition, broader structural features of military life such as hierarchy and uniformity discourage dissent and contribute to power differentials that increase the risk of sexual violence. The military's past denial of the systemic nature of sexual violence and the inadequate handling of sexual harassment and sexual assault complaints have perpetuated the problem. The CAF's current approach to addressing sexual violence focuses on how sexual misconduct undermines opera-tional effectiveness, meaning the military's ability to carry out its missions. While it is positive that the military leadership has finally acknowledged that sexual violence is an endemic problem, its current approach does not go far enough in addressing the features of the military institution that perpetuate sexual violence.

HOW TO UNDERSTAND MILITARY SEXUAL VIOLENCE

Militaries are highly gendered and gender-unequal institutions (Enloe 2000; Goldstein 2001). Most militaries have a long history of "defining and policing the boundaries of women's service" — when, where, and in which roles women can serve, as well as how they can dress (Mathers 2013: 125). In Canada, women make up 15 percent of military personnel, with uneven representation across the organization. They are concentrated in occupations stereotypically associated with femininity — medical, dental, and clerical work — and underrepresented among the senior leadership (Reiffenstein 2007; Davis 2013). The combat arms remain predominantly male and closely tied to a masculinized warrior image. In 2016, only 2.5 percent of CAF personnel in the regular force combat arms and 5.5 percent in the reserve combat arms were women (Department of National Defence and Canadian Armed Forces 2016a). This underrepresentation results from a long history of discrimination against women and resistance to their full integration. The military leadership used to argue that women's presence in the combat arms would undermine unit cohesion and operational effectiveness (Winslow and Dunn 2002). Only in 1989 did the Canadian Human Rights Tribunal order the military to drop its policy barring women from combat occupations, concluding that "there is no risk of failure of performance of combat duties by women sufficient to justify a general exclusionary policy" (Canadian Human Rights Tribunal Decision 1989: 31). Instead, it argued, "emphasis on equality … can strengthen the cohesion which is so highly valued by the Forces. Operational effectiveness is a gender neutral concept" (34).

The problem of sexual violence results not simply from women's historic exclusion from combat occupations and their continued underrepresentation but also from the broader gendered culture of the military. Militaries rely on appeals to masculinity and threats of emasculation to train, motivate, and reward soldiers (Eichler 2014). Basic training is all about "manning up," "killing the woman (and child) within" (Whitworth 2004), and relinquishing personal identity and values in the interests of the group (Whelan 2016). Indoctrination relies on gendered and sexualized rituals that strip new recruits of their identities and remake them into tough masculinized soldiers. Indoctrination also aims to strengthen male bonding through drinking, sexualized banter, and physical exertion, and by appealing to men as the protectors of women and children. Through such practices, the military becomes defined as a heavily masculinized space in which women are constructed as the Other, and characteristics stereotypically associated with femininity, such as weakness, emotion, and vulnerability, are denigrated (Whitworth 2004). This masculinized notion of soldiering limits tolerance towards military members perceived as not fitting in, including women, LGBTQ members, racialized people, and those suffering from injuries such as post-traumatic stress disorder.

Adding to the complexity of the problem of military sexual violence are other features of military organizations. Uniformity, hierarchy, obedience, loyalty to the group, mission before self, and a sense of military superiority over civilian society create a context in which power can be abused and accountability is hard to ensure. Military members are highly dependent on each other. This creates strong bonds but also an environment in which members are reticent to report abuse or to respond effectively to reports of abuse. Though not explicitly about gender, these features reinforce gendered power relations and undermine notions of consent. The military's strict hierarchy is particularly significant as shown by the 2016 Statistics Canada survey. It found that in the CAF, "half (49%) of women who were victims of sexual assault in the past 12 months identified their supervisor or someone of a higher rank as the perpetrator" (Cotter 2016). This is not to say that military members have no agency. Individual members can oppose orders or report wrongdoing. But the broader structural features of militaries constrain these possibilities, as do those of many civilian institutions. Breaking the silence carries the risk of negative repercussions.

FROM DENIAL TO ACKNOWLEDGEMENT

In 1998, reports in *Maclean's* first broke the silence on sexual violence in the Canadian military (O'Hara 1998a, 1998b). In 2014, articles in *Maclean's* and *L'actualité* again brought the issue of sexual assault and sexual harassment in the military to the attention of the Canadian public (Mercier and Castonguay 2014). The stories of the women who came forward highlighted a disturbing lack of action on the part of the military. With growing political pressure and concerns over the military's public standing, the chief of the defence staff ordered internal and external reviews of sexual misconduct in the military (Hutchings 2014).

In April 2015, former Supreme Court of Canada Justice Marie Deschamps released the *External Review into Sexual Misconduct and Sexual Harassment in the Canadian Armed Forces,* also known as the Deschamps Report. It documented a sexualized culture hostile to female and LGBTQ members of the CAF, "characterized by the frequent use of sexualized language, sexual jokes, innuendos, discriminatory comments with respect to the abilities of female members of the military, and … sexual touching" (Deschamps 2015: 14). This prevailing sexualized culture increases the risk of "more serious incidents of sexual harassment and sexual assault" (21). Deschamps argued that addressing sexual misconduct required more than policy change. It required a broader shift in culture; strong leadership; a more robust integration of women, especially among the senior leadership; and the creation of an independent accountability centre to handle sexual assault and harassment complaints by CAF members (vii).

The release of the Deschamps Report turned military sexual violence into an issue of public concern in Canada. Whereas the military leadership had dismissed previous media reports on military sexual violence, saying it resulted from a "few bad apples," it now acknowledged that sexual misconduct was a widespread problem within the forces. The CAF responded to the Deschamps Report with Operation HONOUR, aimed at eliminating sexual violence in the military.

Operation HONOUR has defined the problem of sexual misconduct primarily in relation to operational effectiveness. As the first progress report on Operation HONOUR released in February 2016 stated,

> The presence of harmful and inappropriate sexual behaviour within the Canadian Armed Forces undermines the institution's ability to achieve its mission of defending Canadians and Canadian interests. By corroding the inherent trust and cohesion amongst brothers and sisters in arms that is at the heart of an effective fighting force, such abhorrent conduct undermines nothing less than the Canadian Armed Forces operational capability. (Department of National Defence and Canadian Armed Forces 2016b: 2)

Operation HONOUR introduced measures such as tracking the numbers of reported assaults; improving survivor support and awareness, bystander training, and other prevention initiatives; reviewing the military curriculum; increasing recruitment of women; and creating the independent Sexual Misconduct Response Centre (see Department of National Defence and Canadian Armed Forces 2016b, 2016c). While the military has been able to address several of Deschamps' recommendations, it has not succeeded in initiating a broader cultural shift.

WHAT CHANGE IS NEEDED?

I argue that addressing military sexual violence requires a fundamental cultural shift, one that challenges the gendered and other structural features of the military. Deschamps noted in her review that increasing women's representation, especially among the senior leadership, is one of the key strategies for achieving culture change. The military plans to increase women's representation to 25.1 percent (from 15 percent currently) by 2026 (Government of Canada 2017). For this to ever succeed, effort needs to be put not only into attracting and retaining more women but also, more importantly, into redefining the gendered underpinnings of soldiering.

This requires recruiting soldiers without appealing to masculinity and without invoking the idea that joining the military "makes you a man." Instead of defining the military as a place where masculinity is achieved and celebrated, the military needs to redefine itself as a place where everyone is welcome and where many expressions of masculinity and femininity can be performed without negative repercussions. Soldiers need to be trained without valorizing traits associated with masculinity, such as strength, toughness, and violence over traits associated with femininity such as empathy, vulnerability, and support. The military needs to build a culture of respect and professionalism throughout the forces that does not exclude or undervalue members who do not fit the image of the tough masculinized soldier. It needs to accommodate diverse types of soldiering, not just one implicitly gendered as masculine. Such "re-gendering" or "de-gendering" (Duncanson and Woodward 2016) of the military requires a radical rethinking of military recruitment and training. It may even require rethinking the purpose of militaries, or at least decreasing their emphasis on combat and killing. This reimagining of militaries needs to also go beyond current notions of peacekeeping, which tend to remain tied to masculinized and militarized soldiering (Whitworth 2004).

Moreover, the military needs to reform some of its key features that enable and even encourage the abuse of power. It needs to explore ways to increase the power of individuals and collectivities within its ranks and make the military hierarchy more accountable to those on its lower rungs. The creation of an independent Sexual Misconduct Response Centre as part of Operation HONOUR is a step in the right direction, but more measures need to be taken to allow individuals to bypass the chain of command and avoid negative repercussions for reporting instances of sexual violence. The military also needs to call out high-ranking individuals to signal that everyone in the hierarchy will be held responsible, no matter their rank. While the military leadership has rhetorically committed to eliminating sexual violence, more concerted action and follow-up are needed. Bystander training is another positive measure that has been introduced, but its success will depend on proper implementation and on rewarding those who come forward to speak out.

In the end, the military cannot achieve these changes on its own. Changing its gendered and sexualized culture requires change from within and against the grain. This is the hardest type of culture change to bring about and therefore necessitates external pressure and involvement (English 2016). The media and Canadian public must continue to provide external scrutiny. It is a positive sign that the military decided to repeat the Statistics Canada survey on sexual misconduct two years after the initial 2016 survey, acknowledging that the problem of military sexual violence is ongoing. However, there is a need for greater civilian oversight over the military's handling of sexual assault cases and its progress towards changing its gendered culture. For example, the establishment of a House of Commons oversight committee or other civilian body that is independent and external to the military should be considered. As Deschamps noted in a critical assessment of Operation HONOUR, the Sexual Misconduct Response Centre allows victims to report and seek support but does not go far enough in responding to her recommendation of an independent accountability centre (CBC Radio 2017). True accountability for military sexual violence requires a civilian body that has independence from and authority over the military. Such a body will need to challenge some of the military's gendered and other structural features.

CONCLUSION

I argue that military sexual violence is linked to the gendered and broader structural features of militaries. Features such as hierarchy and conformity, when combined with the privileging of masculinity, create fertile conditions for sexual harassment and sexual assault against women and feminized others, including men who do not conform to the masculinized soldier ideal. Breaking the pattern of sexual violence we see across militaries requires more than better tracking of sexual assault reporting, enhanced survivor support, and a rhetorical commitment to fighting sexual misconduct. Though these are absolutely necessary measures, they are not sufficient. Seriously tackling sexual violence within militaries necessitates, in Canada and elsewhere, changing the gendered and some of the other structural features of militaries. It requires redefining the military's culture, notions of soldiering, and maybe even its purpose. It also requires better civilian oversight over how militaries deal with the problem of sexual violence. These measures need to be part of broader efforts to address the problem of sexual violence across both military and civilian spheres.

PART II

DIS/CONSENTING AGENTS

Chapter 8

SURVIVING WOMAN-TO-WOMAN SEXUAL ASSAULT

KelleyAnne Malinen

This chapter presents narratives of six woman-to-woman sexual assault survivors describing the violence they experienced and the impacts of that violence in the contexts of their lives. Narratives of service provider interviewees are occasionally included as well. Pseudonyms are used throughout for all interviewees. The narratives are organized chronologically into themes that produce a trajectory beginning prior to sexual assault incidents and ending after sexual assault incidents: patterns of sexual violence, sexual assault experiences, help seeking, safer spaces and sacrifices, and working through trauma.

I intend through these themes to communicate some of the ways woman-to-woman sexual violence can occur and profoundly shape the lives of survivors. This simple rationale remains important because, despite approximately forty years of research on various forms of violence between women (Malinen 2014), heteropatriarchal understandings of gender and sexuality continue to obscure the effects, if not the very possibility, of woman-to-woman sexual assault.

While heteropatriarchal norms put women at risk of being sexually violated by men, I take these narratives as evidence that these norms can also be deployed by women. Furthermore, these norms obscure both the fact and harm of women's perpetration where it occurs. Using these thoughts as starting points, I conclude with some observations about how woman-to-woman sexual violence can be understood to fit within the feminist and queer theory of Judith Butler.

"NONE OF IT FELT RIGHT TO ME"

Survivors who participated in this study often experienced multiple incidents of sexually violent behaviour, in physical or emotional forms, perpetrated by their assailants in the period leading up to what they would come to describe as a sexual assault. They recalled confusion over whether their feelings of discomfort were reasonable responses to these patterns of behaviour. Confusion was sometimes amplified by normalizing strategies that were used by perpetrators and facilitated by the social invisibility of women's sexual violence.

In Alice's case, normalization was enabled by a politic that framed woman-to-woman sexuality as empowering, a politic in turn enabled by a social context that does not imagine women's sexual violence as a possibility. As Alice stated,

> PJ had this escort service, and she did this thing where she would bring these women — these workers — over to her apartment. See, everything about it was — my apartment faced her apartment. There was a window well, and she could look into my apartment and I could look into her apartment. Our apartments were right next to each other but there was a sort of well space between them. And so, she would deliberately — at least it seemed to me — she would deliberately bring home these workers. Some of them were strippers and some of them were prostitutes, and most of them were very beautiful. And she would kinda tease me with that and try to make me really jealous. And so, you say, "Okay, I can't deal with this, I'm gonna put down my window shades," and then you get a phone call saying, "Why are you taking your window shades down?" So that was part of the abuse, but it was very, very confusing. It was *so* confusing because it was all women. The mentality of the feminist circles in the city was sort of — I have nothing against sex workers, I've

done it myself — but it was this sort of "Wow!" you know, that "they're *empowering* each other."

For Laura, normalization took the form of insistence that the sexual harassment she was experiencing was a funny joke, again enabled by a social context that does not take seriously women's sexual violence:

> In high school, I met this group of people that lived on the outskirts of town. There was a brother and a sister, Patricia, and another brother and, you know, a couple of my friends. It was just like, the party house. It was the place to go to escape and have fun. There had been a lot of advances from Patricia, but I wasn't willing to give up that environment. So, it made me very uncomfortable — I made it clear it made me very uncomfortable. My friends all knew. It made them uncomfortable. But the family, like, the brother and sister and her, would always laugh it off. It would be a joke. She'd make comments, like, comments about my breasts or about, you know, what I was wearing that day, or "let me squeeze your butt," slap my butt, stuff like that, and I honestly didn't get it. None of it felt right to me, and I know I snapped back on her many a time. I'd snap back and then I wouldn't see her for a while.

"I COULDN'T MOVE, YOU KNOW?"

Some survivors described experiences that they did not view as sexual assault but that seemed to fit definitions of sexual assault under Canadian law, suggesting that barriers to recognition can shape the perceptions of survivors themselves. The passages below, however, refer to incidents described by survivor interviewees as sexual assault or rape. Each of the following narratives recollects perpetrator violence, including physical force, emotional force, intoxication, and/or isolation. Each also includes survivor expressions of non-consent, including physical and emotional disengagement, verbal expressions like "I don't think it's a good idea" and "stop," and/or physical forms of resistance.

When we eventually got to the bar, I was very drunk, and I was leaning against Elaine on the couch. My mind started spiralling like it does before you pass out, and she got on top of me and started making out with me.... Then, at the end of the evening, she wanted to sleep over at my place.... She started to get frustrated and angry. I just remember being outside of this bar and her being like, "You have to give me an answer!" and I'm like, "I don't think it's a good idea." ... It's hazy exactly what was said, but she ended up at my place.... It only lasted, like, ten minutes and I didn't want it to happen. Near the beginning, like the first two minutes, I guess she knew it, and she got mad at me. I was really scared, so I just kind of went along with it. I remember her being on top of me and I wasn't interested in what was going on. I don't remember exactly what she said, but I know she was angry. I was like, "I have this angry woman on top of me, what am I going to do?" (Nora)

Our group was going to meet up and watch something on TV, but when I got there it was just her and I. We were sitting on her couch in the living room, and I was starting to feel really uncomfortable because she was starting to, like, put her hand on me and make advances. And so I called my friend and was telling her, you know, "She keeps touching me and I don't feel comfortable, and when are you guys coming over?" My friend said to me, "She cancelled." Patricia had cancelled with all the friends, so that's how I found out nobody was coming. At that point, Patricia got on top of me with my friend still on the phone and put her hand down my shirt and down my pants and I was telling her, "Get off! Stop touching me!" You know, making it very clear, but she had me pinned. I was pinned down.... The only thing I could say was, "No! Don't do that! Don't touch me!" And that's when she sexually assaulted me.... She did physical damage to me as well. I went to the hospital, because I was bleeding very badly after the assault. (Laura)

So what happened was, I heard the key go into the lock. It was, like, 10:30, I was reading in bed, and she came into my place, into my little bedroom, and said she was going to teach me a lesson, and that this was the lesson. I got up and was like, "Why are you in my — what's going on?" But she grabbed me by the arms, and then pinned me down, and proceeded to make love to me, in a very PJ-like way — very dominant. So I told her *I didn't want to do it.* I said, "I think we have a bad relationship going, and I think we need to take a break." It was so long ago, I can't remember every specific word I said, but I can remember resisting verbally and trying to coax her out of trying to make love with me. Because after my verbal resistance she wouldn't stop, I started to struggle. And that's where what I think of as a form of rape, or sexual assault, started. I resisted. I'd squirm, I'd pull my arms back, I'd tell her "I don't want this!" and "Give me my key back!" And then it got *very physical.* She kept me down very strongly with both her arms and her legs, so I had no ability to resist.... She managed to hold my arms over my head.... When she'd eventually gotten what she wanted and she was done, she got up. I remember very specifically she was wearing these corduroy, baggy pants, her pulling them up, and it was so much like a man, you know? She was standing over me and she said — and again, this is not exact words — but while she was zipping up her zipper and her button and the whole thing, tucking in her shirt, basically cleaning herself up, she said, "There, I've taught you a lesson. See? You wanted it." And then she left. (Alice)

They admitted Tanya into the detox unit, and she phoned me and let me know. So I said okay, I'd come and visit her. It was a public place, so I went in. She was in her own room and she got up and closed the door, you know, to talk. We were talking for, I don't know, about a half an hour or forty-five minutes and I got up to use the toilet, and she came in after me and she assaulted me while I was on the toilet. She penetrated me ... and held me down. I couldn't move, you know? She held me down against the back of the toilet.... I just kept saying [whispers] "Tanya, you need to get off of me, Tanya, stop, just stop." (Leanne)

Whereas victim non-consent is frequently placed under doubt in sexual assault cases, the physical capacity of the perpetrator to overwhelm the victim is generally accepted in man-to-woman incidents. This is not the case when perpetrators are women. In the above narratives, we notice survivors specifying the ways in which their bodies were immobilized, with phrases like "I was pinned down," "she held me down very strongly," and "I couldn't move, you know?" These precisions in the narratives of survivor interviewees seem to respond pre-emptively to disbelief. In these cases, disbelief is particularly likely to arise because women are not understood as having the physical power or psychological inclination to sexually assault, and because of an ideology that positions women as sexual gatekeepers. To the extent that women are not understood as having the physical strength to inflict sexual assault, those who experience sexual assault inflicted by women are likely to be seen as not having resisted, and therefore are disbelieved.

"I HAD NO ONE TO TURN TO"

As indicated by the MSVU Feminist Collective in Chapter 6, survivor speech always risks encountering the retraumatizing violence of denial. The memories that appear in this section attest to specific barriers to validation rooted in gender norms and expectations and confronted by survivors of woman-to-woman sexual violence. As Ardath Whynacht puts it in Chapter 12, women are simply not legible as aggressors. While not all survivor participants sought formalized supports following sexual assaults, those who did were often let down by service providers.

> When I finally got interviewed by the police they were really putting doubt out there. Like, "Really? What were you doing there?" You know, like, "Why didn't you leave?" You know, like, "How strong was she really?" Things like that, just very — I felt very backed into a corner, like, why am I even doing this? For me it was very uncomfortable. It was almost as if they looked at me immediately and as soon as they heard that it was a female, everything went downhill from there. (Laura)

> I got out the phone book and I got out my phone, and I dialled

the hotline and literally had a conversation where the person answered and I said, "I've been raped," and she proceeded to ask the proper questions. And when I used the pronoun "she" for my assailant, the woman on the other end got indignant … and told me that she didn't appreciate the prank and not to call back. So, I was really, really just beside myself. I had no one to turn to.… I was just shocked that there was no help.… I just hung up and I — I cried. (Alice)

Alice was alone among participants in finding effective support services within a short period after the assault. Soon after her initial effort to obtain help through the hotline, which had retraumatized her, a lesbian-centred intimate partner violence support group was created.

The narratives above demonstrate damaging incompetency when it comes to dealing with woman-to-woman sexual violence. Encounters with such incompetence can greatly alter the trajectories of survivors' lives. The following service provider narrative about the police response to a survivor resonates with Paris Perry's recollection of police indifference to an attack by a client (Chapter 11):

Tara came in [to the addiction treatment centre] one day just absolutely a bloody mess, bruised, very fearful, very shaky, not like her.… Eventually she informed us that she had got herself into a social situation where she was using with a group of these women, her ex-partner being one of them.… She got badly raped and in her time of fighting back, the ex-partner, Janice, was punching her and scratching her and broke her nose and did a lot of damage to her.… When the police arrived, it was *definitely* a burden. It was almost something you felt like you had to apologize to them for.… My co-worker and I looked at each other and just, without saying it, "This isn't going to be good." And it wasn't.… You could see the life just leaving her, because she stood up against a group of her peers knowing probably none of them would want anything to do with her, probably would look for some sort of retribution. So then she was left in a situation where she was very vulnerable and feeling unsafe.… She was just doing cocaine and crack before. Now she's doing anything and everything including solvents and injecting. Physically, she looks like she could die at any time.… She had somewhat of a relation with her family prior to. Now she's got *nothing*. Nothing at all. (Caitlyn)

"SO I WAS GONE"

During fieldwork, I was struck by the strategizing, time, social networks, and pure luck required by survivors to create distance between themselves and the perpetrators. It became clear that this distance was required for survivors to feel safe — or at least safer — in the aftermath of their assault experiences. Establishing this space consistently involved sacrifice: of housing, of community, of family and friend relationships, of employment and education. Narratives in this section draw attention to the losses incurred by survivors as they worked toward finding safety and re-establishing their lives.

For Laura, the "party house" where she was sexually assaulted by Patricia had been the place she went to escape sexual abuse perpetrated by her brother (who was himself a survivor). Once she was sexually assaulted at the party house, she had no safe place left to go. The party house belonged to Patricia's family, and Patricia's sibling attended Laura's school.

It was very strained, very awkward at school.… Patricia's brother would say things to my friends, because he was still friends with them.… Just, you know, "I can't believe she charged her!" … Just, little things I'd hear … and feel very uncomfortable about. I started skipping a lot, sleeping a lot. I had to go on medication for depression and then dropped out of school.… It was about January, so I dropped out until summertime. And then through the summer, I didn't want to go back. So they had just opened up this new program for the region, which was a classroom for kids who struggled in normal systems. There were two teachers there who would support correspondence studies, so I joined that … and that's how I ended up graduating high school. (Laura)

Leanne secretly prepared and then moved to a different province in order to re-establish her life:

I had to leave the community. I applied to come to school and she [Tanya] knew that I was doing that but I sort of just kept it hidden and didn't say anything once I got accepted. I tidied everything up by July, I think, of the year, so I was gone. And then what I did ... was I just got a plain post office box, an unlisted phone number. (Leanne)

Christmas with her was hell ... in the sense that I had two weeks off school. I wasn't happy about that.... I had some frigging peace when I went to school. But during those two weeks, it was two more weeks with her [mother] all over me.... It wasn't just sexual abuse, it was verbal violence, physical violence.... I had a friend who was in the same building where I lived.... After the Christmas holiday, I said, "Manon, I can't take it anymore, I'm going to run away, I'm not okay here anymore." ... I lived *in terror*, real terror. I was *afraid* of my mother.... My friend took me to see a social worker, and they took me out of there. I arrived there at nine o'clock in the morning, and at two in the afternoon, they took me out.... I did a couple of centres because, well, when they took me out of my mother's they had to put me in temporary care. The woman where I was ... called the social worker. She said, "Get her out of here, because that's a good little girl, and she's going to turn bad," because I was with delinquents, right? So then, they put me in a closed centre. They locked the doors at night. So I said to my social worker, "I don't belong here. I never did anything wrong." After that, they put me in a foster home for girls, and then I was happy. (Dominique)

"I WOULDN'T BE HERE TODAY IF I HADN'T BEEN THROUGH THIS STUFF"

Survivors spoke of the fear and sometimes anger that resulted from sexual assault and other experiences of violence and abuse. When interviews took place, some participants felt they had moved past these experiences more than others did.

I dreamed for a long time that I struck her, but never with my hand It was always with my feet. I spit on her, and it was my feet. And the more she screamed, the more I said, "Come on!" and I kept on giving it to her, you know. And even still today with all of the healing I have in my body, with the — you know, with the help I have and everything, I best not come face-to-face with her. I don't know what I'd do. (Dominique)

Any relationships that I got into, which were very difficult for me, I couldn't — I'm just going to say this — it wasn't until the past couple months, literally, so from that day to this day, where I could actually let someone's hands get close to my vagina. (Laura)

It's been definitely a growth process. It's definitely taken its time. Now I'm at a place where my emotions are more safely controlled. I can cry in situations that are worth crying for, get angry in situations that are worth getting angry for, or worth being happy for, or being fearful for. (Jade)

A number of participants suggested that healing from the sexual assaults they had experienced involved making meaning out of victimization. Processes of meaning-making ranged from talk therapy to using their understandings of trauma to help others.

I wrote some poetry, just to kind of come to terms with the feelings, because there's something about the physical pain, you know, and the emotional pain that gets really sort of intertwined, you know?... And then I found a really good therapist who helped me release a lot of that emotional pain that I was holding, because you just hold it in your body. (Leanne)

I wouldn't be here today, helping these women, if I hadn't been through this stuff. You know? And my whole life's work, all of that trauma that's happened to me, it lives with me every day but it lives in me to a point where now I can help other people. (Laura)

CONCLUSION

The emphasis on transforming trauma into a capacity to help others, exemplified by Laura's narrative, ocurred in other participants' narratives and appeared to be a primary motive for many to participate in this study. Most interviewees sought reassurance that their input would ultimately be used to help other survivors of woman-to-woman sexual assault find recognition and support.

It is important to remember that experiences of sexual violence differ in many ways, including the form the violence takes, victim and perpetrator identities and relationship, whether and which traumatic effects result, and how the experiences shape the survivor's life. However, not only did those who chose to participate in my study recall a diversity of experiences, they also constituted a very specific group. Because they responded to a call for participants who had experienced woman-to-woman sexual assault, we can suppose that all found the label "sexual assault" fitting to their experiences. All were able to muster the time and energy for participation, and all were sufficiently free from controlling partners to meet me. All were motivated to share their stories. Our conversation was the first time Leanne spoke of her sexual assault experience, even though she had received considerable therapy to deal with abuses she had suffered. She is certainly not alone in her silence. Given the invalidating and even incredulous responses that every survivor participant had received on at least one occasion, it is noteworthy that these women continued to tell their stories at all.

In the context of a volume that places an emphasis on the impacts of colonial heteropatriarchy, we must ask: How do these women's stories fit in relationship to said social structures? In what remains, I explore two threads that render heteropatriarchy foundational to the experiences of woman-to-woman sexual assault survivors.

Specific Barriers to Recognition

Heteropatriarchal society represents women, especially proper white women, as weak and unthreatening. Heteropatriarchy suggests that men have sexual appetites, which women arouse; hence, Debra Paris Perry recalls in this volume that her grandmother warned the girls, "Don't go pickin' blueberries by yourself, because if you do the boys will get you and it will be your fault." Nobody ever told the boys, "Keep your fuckin' hands to yourself," Paris Perry explains. Women act as gatekeepers in this sexual economy, withholding or granting consent.

Furthermore, rape myths ensure that women are read as having granted consent in any number of ways without actually having done so. We can again reflect here on the MSVU Feminist Collective's response to Judge Lenehan and also on the legal strategies of perpetrator defence lawyers, explored by Andrea Zanin and Dorothy Grant, which convince judges or juries that "she asked for it." This gendering has effects on the levels of both action and perception. On the one hand, due to gender-based socialization, men are certainly more likely than women to sexually assault people. On the other hand, we are socialized such that we have difficulty perceiving sexual assaults that are committed by women. When asked what single message it was most important to send out about woman-to-woman sexual assault, all but one participant responded with some variation of the phrase "that it happens."

When I began this study, I was repeatedly asked — mostly by puzzled men — how it was possible for one woman to sexually assault another. The fact that lesbians, bisexuals, and other queer women exist had apparently not translated for these men into an understanding that women can take sexual initiative and act upon one another sexually, let alone do so without consent. The imagining of such a possibility for some men was precluded by interference from the apparently overwhelming fantasy of "having" two women simultaneously. Many men are eager to say that all heterosexual men share this fantasy, somehow expecting this to be new, interesting, or useful information.

Even among those who recognize the physical possibility of women's bodies engaging in a sexually violent way, there can be a failure to acknowledge the harms that woman-perpetrated violence can cause. In this context, some people are able to imagine a woman using her body to perform a non-consensual act without being able to imagine that such an act could produce harm. Our bodies are understood to affirm men's autonomy and status (many men feel entitled to this); our bodies are subject to judgement as objects; our bodies may provide comfort. Our bodies may outrage male entitlement through a withholding of consent but — or so goes the assumption — do not actively take away autonomy, negate status, or do harm the way a penis can. Hence, some people understand in principle that a woman may hold another woman down so that she cannot move in order to physically penetrate her body, yet remain fundamentally oblivious to the fact that this violence *does* anything. In the exasperated words of a service provider participant who was responding to the ways that gendered ideology interferes with recognition of harm: "This is a human relationship, and this behaviour causes *this* effect for another person, right? It has *this* effect." The narratives reported in this chapter communicate some of the many effects woman-to-woman sexual violence has in the lives of survivors.

The Logic of Sexual Assault

The ways our culture encourages us to think about men and women lie at the heart of the heteropatriarchal logic of sexual assault. Sexual assault can only emerge in a context where some people feel entitled to do as they wish to the bodies of others, regardless of what those others think or feel. Those socialized to such entitlement in our culture are typically men. In *Gender Trouble* — the 1992 work that propelled Judith Butler to queer theory fame — Butler argues that in their own masculine performances, women draw on and resist heterosexual culture. Key to this argument is the understanding that the association between men and those elements of culture understood as masculine is cultural rather than natural. Any person — man, woman, or non-binary — who presents as masculine, whether more permanently or more temporarily, more fully or more partially, is engaged in the performance of a cultural script. Masculinity does not belong to men, and femininity does not belong to women; masculinity and femininity can each be performed or embodied in various ways by people across genders.

In her explorations of this area, Butler's focus was typically on positive feminist and queer potentials implicit in performances of gender that transgress our expectations. However, on occasion, for example in *Undoing Gender*, Butler (2004) suggests that women can take up masculinity in politically regressive ways, such as by enacting sexual violence towards other women. Butler would agree that norms expressed through non-consensual infliction of violence should not be reproduced at all.

This form of queering heteropatriarchy moves toward neither non-violent nor democratic forms of life (this argument is made at length in Malinen 2012).

So where does woman-to-woman sexual violence hang in the web of heteropatriarchy? In short, to counter the cultural antecedents of sexual violence inclusively and thoroughly, we must find ways to challenge the heteropatriarchal norms that are consistent with sexual violence. These norms put women at greatest risk of being sexually violated by men, they can be taken up by women, and they obscure the fact and harm of women's perpetration where it occurs.

Chapter 9

POWER STRUGGLES OVER THE SEXUALITIES OF INDIVIDUALS WITH INTELLECTUAL DISABILITIES

Alan Santinele Martino

It is often assumed that people with intellectual disabilities (ID) are unable to manage their own sexual decision-making (Hollomotz and The Speakup Committee 2008). On the one hand, people with ID are often seen as "eternal children," without sexual desires. On the other hand, these individuals are believed to have "excessive" sexualities that must be restricted (Esmail et al. 2010; McRuer 2015). These two conflicting perspectives create barriers to the sexual autonomy of people with ID (Gill 2015; Kulick and Rydström 2015). The existing literature on disability and sexuality tends to focus on sex education and staff training as ways to enhance the sexual decision-making of people with ID (Gill 2015). However, such trainings tend not to move beyond the prevalent perspective that sexuality will land people with ID in trouble. In contrast, in this chapter I explore how direct care workers affect the sexual and romantic lives of individuals with ID and how care workers' responses to the sexual and romantic lives of clients with ID are shaped by care workers' employers and clients' guardians.

METHODS

For this study, I interviewed five individuals with ID who were their own legal guardians and six direct care workers. By interviewing participants with ID who were their own guardians, I avoided having to obtain informed consent from the legal guardians in addition to the participants — an obligation that would have encumbered the study significantly (Lennox et al. 2005; Nind 2008). It is important to recognize that, as compared to those who are not their own legal guardians, participants had considerable opportunity for sexual and romantic expression and evolution. However, the sexual autonomy of these participants was often hard-won.

Participants with ID included four men and one woman, from 23 to 42 years of age. All participants identified as Canadian, white, and heterosexual. At the time of the interviews, two participants had been married for over five years, and three were single; one of them was divorced. Two were living together independently in a family-owned house, one was living with roommates, one was living with a roommate companion,[1] and one was living in a rented house with the support of a direct care worker. All of these participants had finished high school, and one was working on his bachelor's degree. Three participants were self-employed, one was employed, and one was unemployed.

Consistent with studies that have examined care work as a gendered form of labour (e.g., Wilson et al. 2011), direct care worker interviewees included five women and one man. Workers were aged 23 to 49 years and drawn from five agencies, where they had been employed for periods ranging from two months to twenty-seven years. They included permanent and relief workers who provided overnight assistance at group homes, respite services to parents and caregivers, and supports to individuals with ID in community activities such as shopping for groceries and attending community events. Four participants identified as Canadian and white, one identified as Southeast Asian, and one as Latin American. Three identified as heterosexual, one as gay, one as bisexual, and one as undeclared. Education levels varied; three held bachelor's degrees, two were current undergraduate students, and one participant was working towards a master's degree.

Although small in scale, this study allowed me to delve into the complex experiences of some individuals with ID and some direct care workers as they relate to the sexualities of people with ID. However, the reader should keep in mind that people with ID and direct care workers are diverse groups living in diverse contexts, and members of each population may vary in the degree to which they relate to my findings (Finlay 2006).

FINDINGS AND DISCUSSION

Power struggles emerged as a recurring and overarching theme through-out the research. All participants explicitly or implicitly discussed power relations, decision-making capacity, constraints, and resistance. Participants with ID talked about their struggles in developing sexual and romantic relationships, gaining privacy, and dealing with control-ling workers and/or guardians. Additionally, this group of self-advocates[2] talked about how being their own guardians allowed them to assert more sexual agency relative to those under guardianship orders. Power strug-gles centred around the autoerotic practices, dating opportunities, and reproductive health of participants with ID.

Power Struggles Experienced
by Individuals with Intellectual Disabilities

With respect to their romantic and sexual lives, individuals with ID, regardless of their guardianship status, are often denied the right to make decisions, take risks, make mistakes, and learn from them (Koller 2000). However, this research speaks to the fact that that those with ID also resist the control people around them attempt to impose. The notion of power struggle was first introduced by Jeremy, then in his twenties, as he discussed his relationship with his landlady:

> She wasn't paid staff, but it kind of illustrates that power struggle like, she was the main one on the contract for the rental place and she said my room had to be like clean and stuff to the point that I had no privacy. Like she would be in my room checking it out constantly.

Because they are seen as childlike and in need of protection, people with ID are often not granted space or autonomy (Gesser, Nuernberg, and

Toneli 2014; Hollomotz and The Speakup Committee 2008). For Jeremy, having his landlady enter his room without warning was a significant barrier to the masturbation and consumption of pornography that were his main sexual outlets. Illustrating his capacity and willingness to resist, Jeremy recalled,

> I told her that "my room is my room, you can't tell me what to do with my room or else I am gonna leave." She kept saying that [the room needed to be clean and could not contain any pornography], and I'm just like, "I'm done [laughs]. I am outta there, this is not a good place for me," and it's that, where she thought she had authority over me, and it's like, "no, you don't so I am outta here."

There is a tension between the need to receive services and the surveillance that comes with staff who are, in Jeremy's words, "above you all the time." In addition, Jeremy's story shows that individuals with ID and their paid staff may have conflicting values about appropriate forms of sexual expression. To resolve these power struggles, Jeremy moved temporarily to his parents' house while seeking a new living arrangement. At the time of the interview, he was sharing a house with other men in his own age group.

Anthony spoke about similar power struggles over control of his living space. At the time of the interview, he lived at a house on his own with the support of a personal assistant living next door. However, in the past, he had lived in a group home where the doors were locked after a 10 p.m. curfew and visitors were always prohibited. This had limited his opportunities to socialize, meet potential romantic and sexual partners, and engage in flirtation, hook-ups, and courtship. Anthony moved out of the group home and personally hired a worker.

Samantha too found her romantic opportunities limited by those around her. She attempted a few romantic relationships in school, but recalled, "It was rough. I would be in and out of a relationship within like a week to two weeks.... I kept getting hurt. When they found out I had a disability it's like, 'Okay, I'll just use you and I'm off.'" In an apparent effort to "protect" her from "getting hurt," her family became a barrier to sexual expression and practices. Samantha spoke about how her parents and brothers had discouraged previous boyfriends she had introduced to them:

I noticed, every time I said to my parents, "I am seeing someone," the relationship would sour two months later so I got, you know, if I don't say anything to my parents right away, maybe this relationship will work out.... [It's hard] when you're the youngest of three and you got two older brothers that protect you.

The impulse to protect family members with ID may have a basis in the fact that people with ID are disproportionately likely to be victims of abuse, both in care and in the community (Murphy 2003; Sequeira and Halstead 2001). Estimates vary greatly, ranging from 10 to 80 percent, of the proportion of individuals with ID who will experience sexual abuse at some point in their lives (Hollomotz 2011). Furthermore, research affirms that parents struggle to find a balance between allowing their children with ID to make their own sexual decisions and protecting their children with ID from heartaches or from "getting in trouble" (Löfgren-Mårtenson 2004). Women with ID like Samantha tend to be viewed as particularly in need of protection and may therefore experience greater levels of social isolation and dependency on caregivers (Grabois 2001).

One common justification for inhibiting the sexual expression of people with ID is the assumed risk of pregnancy, coupled with the assumption they will be unable to parent effectively. William recalled,

This isn't my current worker, but when I got married the worker [said something like], "So we need to get you to the health unit and all that" ... because "oh you can't have children, you don't know how to take — you're not capable of that."

Similar to other parents with ID (Ignagni and Schormans 2016), William perceived himself and his partner at the time as having had the potential to parent effectively with the right supports in place:

We wanted children. I mean, anybody wants children. I mean, you might have a bit of a tougher time supporting it, but there is family, friends, people who will support you. So I think that was our dream and it didn't last long enough.... I honestly think there really is a lot of drawbacks for people with disabilities. People think, "Oh you can't have children."

William and his wife refused to go to the clinic or use birth control. "That's the luxury for me as I am my own guardian.... We ignored [the worker] and did our own thing," he said, adding, "She didn't preclude us from ever having children, but the fact that people were saying 'you shouldn't' or 'you should get on birth control' is really the issue." Like an echo from the past, William's narrative demonstrates the continued efforts to prevent people with ID from parenthood. Up until 1972, the province of Alberta had formal legal eugenics practices aimed at "containing" the sexualities of disabled people (Grekul, Krahn, and Odynak 2004). Eugenicists claimed that social problems were genetically inherited, and advocated for marriage regulation as well as selective breeding (Malacrida 2008). Alberta was responsible for 90 percent of more than 2,800 cases of involuntary sterilization of disabled people in Canada from 1928 to 1972 (Grekul, Krahn, and Odynak 2004). Recent studies continue to demonstrate the legacies of eugenics in shaping the intimate lives of disabled people today (e.g., Eugenics to Newgenics 2018).

Power Struggles Experienced by Direct Care Workers

Historically, direct care workers have held considerable cultural authority to control the sexual expressions of the people with ID they support (Goble 1999). This study shows that power imbalances remain embedded in relationships between workers and clients. However, this study also demonstrates that some workers struggle to negotiate the politics of their roles in the sexual lives of clients with ID.

Like other care workers, Celine faced pressure to accommodate the expectations, regulations, and values of different social actors, institutions, agreements, and policies. She stated,

> As a person, you don't feel like you should have power over this other person necessarily ... but you're filling this institutional role, where ... you represent the organization, you represent the guardian, you represent the policies, you represent the rules, you represent all this paperwork and red tape.

Most workers reported feeling apprehensive about the sexual desires of their clients, mainly due to the conflicting expectations of the actors in their clients' networks. They reported fear of "getting in trouble" for not responding to their client's sexual desires and practices in the manner prescribed by the organizations they worked for or the guardians or family members of their clients. They spoke about tensions between the policies and expectations of their organizations, the perceived beliefs and attitudes of guardians, their own beliefs and practices, and the expectations and desires of their clients.

Some female care workers reported being the objects of sexual and/or romantic feelings from clients, which sometimes evoked great complexity. Celine, for example, spoke about instances in which Brian had erections while receiving care:

> The guy who I told you about, he has a very religious family, and he was young when I was working with him, he was early twenties. Very sexually frustrated. I really liked working with him. He was a great guy, but sometimes I felt incredible guilt being a young female working with him because it just reminded him about how sexually frustrated he was. So despite we had a great dynamic, and his roommate and I got along really well.… I could tell especially bathing and like transfer, and getting dressed or any of the more personal stuff.

In the above passage, the physical proximity and intimacy that can be essential to direct care work may be seen as interacting with gender socialization such that Celine saw her youth and femaleness as causing sexual frustration for Brian and felt responsible and therefore guilty with respect to Brian's sexual frustration. A man engaged in direct care work would be unlikely to experience the same nexus of interactions, thoughts, and emotions — which is by no means to suggest that Celine ought to have responded otherwise. While Celine's feelings of guilt were unfortunate, her feelings of care were clearly well placed.

This direct care worker's analysis of the situation extended beyond the micro level, moving into the institutional context. Celine understood Brian's lack of sexual outlet as largely a product of his familial situation and the conservative values he had inherited. In this context, she saw Brian's sexual and emotional vulnerability:

Because he was so conservative and his family was so conservative, I didn't bring it to attention with him because he wasn't in a place where he was in control. He had no control over the fact that I had to bathe him, he had no control over his body, and no control over the social situation. And I mean, most people are never gonna end up in a social situation like this so it's uncharted to navigate, but I just didn't bring attention to it. Some ... people may be embarrassed, maybe some people won't wanna work with him again, but I am — for me, in my mind, it's like, "Whatever, an erection." They happen, right? It's whatever, right?

Because Celine was untroubled by Brian's erection, she may have been able to navigate his physical signs of arousal in a way that minimized any feelings of embarrassment, guilt, or shame. She described her approach as follows:

> Keep talking to him. Keep asking him questions. He at first seemed embarrassed ... the first time, but then when I just kept powering through and didn't even blink, so to speak, like just — 'cause I really did not want him to feel uncomfortable or embarrassed because he — if anything, I just felt bad. I felt bad that ... I wasn't in a position to help him more, that I couldn't suggest getting a prostitute for him or something because his family would never approve. And I didn't even wanna talk to him about it 'cause I didn't wanna give him false hope.... My goal was to not embarrass him, that was my main goal, to make him feel comfortable and — and not judged.

While Marina expressed similarly warm sentiments toward a client who "would get sweet on" his direct care workers, her narrative focuses on the drawing of boundaries in a way that Celine's does not. Marina spoke about a time when a client unexpectedly kissed her neck:

> I got kissed on the neck [laughs]. Yeah, I got kissed, really quick, yeah, and I said, "Excuse me?" and he said, "Oh." So that was the guy who used to go, you know, he would start touching himself and we'd say, "No, you need to go to your room." But one time

he was looking — he needed to look in the freezer and then he kissed my neck and I said, "Excuse me?" and he said, "Oh, oh I am sorry," and I said, "Yeah, that's good, 'cause that's my neck, you are not supposed to kiss my neck" [laughs].

Marina chose not to report this instance to her organization as she also pointed to the challenges and frustrations experienced by people with ID who want to have relationships. Like Celine, Marina seemed to speak to power struggles as she suggested that the client's parents could have been one of the factors preventing the young man from having romantic relationships.

> We knew in that — in that environment there were other direct service workers that he was, that he would get sweet on, and so yeah, we would just say, "That's not appropriate. I don't want you kissing my neck" [laughs]. I'd say like, "Do I kiss your neck?" He would say, "No." "Okay, so I don't want you kissing mine" [laughs]. He probably was an individual who would have been served well if he had a relationship with someone, sadly. He probably needed that, and I don't know whether his guardian ever allowed that. I suspect not but he probably would have a nice relationship. You know, he was healthy, positive, happy person. He was polite. So, I don't know if she [his guardian] ever dealt with that or not.

Direct care workers perceived family members and guardians to be the ultimate decision-makers when determining what forms of sexual expression were permissible. As Marina put it, "Guardians have a lot of power, a lot of power, and ultimately, we only have a voice to the degree that we can offer suggestions, and if the guardian says 'no,' it's a no." The responsibilities given to care workers often include merely reporting incidents and then observing and enforcing decisions made by guardians and high-level management regarding their clients' sexual expression and practices. For example, Celine talked about how all the women with ID she had supported had (knowingly or unknowingly) received birth control. She shared, "It's frustrating and tiring to constantly deal with things that you disagree with and then have to enforce things you disagree with.... The overmedication was a big one for me. I disagree with that."

CONCLUSIONS

Both individuals with ID and direct care workers see the sexual expression of people with ID as a site of power struggle. Further research about how care workers who would have wished to negotiate client sexuality, as well as about how client sexuality arises in the context of client-worker relationships, would be useful. Ideally, support workers would feel empowered to advocate for the sexual rights of their clients and enable their clients to pursue sexual and romantic opportunities.

Overall, this research suggests that protectionism, even when coming from a genuine place of concern and care, can lead to the silencing of those we want to protect because we perceive them to be vulnerable. It is important to understand that people with disabilities have agency, have romantic and sexual desires, and make decisions based on their own understandings of the world. William puts it in words likely to ring true for any dater: "It is hard to date," but nevertheless, "there's a lot that we learn" from those experiences. "A lot of people do make mistakes, but everyone learns and moves on."

Chapter 10

SEX WORK AND THE PARADOX OF CONSENT

Meredith Ralston

Double binds and double standards in relation to sexuality are familiar territory for many women and other disadvantaged groups. In this chapter, I describe one of the most egregious double binds — one having to do with female sex workers and the issue of sexual consent or lack thereof. In particular, there are two very different ways that consent is negated in the lives of sex workers. On the one hand, many activists and scholars in the anti-prostitution movement believe that women are incapable of consenting to prostitution. Framing prostitution as inherent victimization and conflating sex work with sex trafficking, they believe that no one can consent to their own exploitation, which is why they call sex workers "prostituted women." On the other hand, it is commonly believed that in paying money for sexual services, the client acquires the right to do anything he wants to the sex worker. In other words, sex workers confront two opposing and equally erroneous assumptions: first, that women can't consent to sex work (i.e., they lack agency) and second, that sex workers cannot withhold consent to sex (i.e., they are unrapeable).

When I began researching prostitution, sex work, and sex trafficking, generally focusing on the experiences of bar girls in the Philippines and survival sex workers in Canada, my view on prostitution was very negative and my research emphasized the exploitation I saw within the industry. Meeting bar girls as young as 16 and knowing that one of the young women I had met died of HIV-related causes made me deeply suspicious of the generally white male Westerners who were the girls' main customers. The research in the Philippines became the basis of my film *Hope in Heaven*, which was broadcast on CBC in 2007 as *Selling Sex in Heaven*. Following the release of that film, I was challenged by several online escorts based in the United States to broaden my outlook on selling and buying sex. In their response to the sex tourism film, they emphasized that what I was describing was not voluntary sex work between consenting adults but rather involuntary sex trafficking or child sexual exploitation. Eventually meeting some of these women led me to write, direct, and produce a second film, entitled *Selling Sex*. In making that film I interviewed six former or currently working escorts and two of their clients, three sex work researchers, four anti-prostitution activists, and two sex surrogates. The research presented here emerges from these interviews and reflects my own struggles to understand sex work differently. The sex workers were (or had been) online escorts and had experience working in brothels and massage parlours, and one also had experience working on the street. They were all white women, aged 30 to 55, and all but one had some college education. Two identified as lesbian and four as straight. All were cisgender. Four were married, and two were single and practised polyamory. None of the women had children at the time of the interviews but since then one has had twins. They were from Toledo, Detroit, Las Vegas, Los Angeles, and New York. I met my main character, Lucy, (all names have been changed) at a workshop for sex work activists and met the others through Lucy and through sex work organizations.

Meeting these women forced the evolution in my own thinking from an anti-prostitution point of view to what I now consider a more nuanced pro-decriminalization stance. Using carceral strategies to deal with commercial sex between consenting adults only harms the female sex worker who chooses for a variety of reasons to do sex work (Bruckert and Parent 2018; Durisin, Van der Meulen, and Bruckert 2018; Mac and Smith 2018; Maynard 2017; Balfour and Comack 2014). More controversially, Lucy, an eighteen-year veteran of the escort business, helped me make sense of what she calls the "value" of sex work. From her point of view, sexuality and physical intimacy are important aspects of human experience that should be valued and embraced, but, unfortunately, not everyone has access to unpaid physical intimacy. Sex work is not valued because sexuality is not valued as it should be. Furthermore, she claimed, women's sexuality, in particular, is still highly stigmatized. In speaking with these women, I came to understand that the stigma against sex workers and sex work perpetuates the stigma against women's sexuality in general, and in the film and a forthcoming book, I explore the unintended consequences of marginalizing and stigmatizing sex workers. The need to understand why my previous position on sex work was misguided and often unhelpful to sex workers led me to see how problematic prohibitionist[1] feminism can be. The marginalization and stigmatization of sex workers can be created even by those who want to help or rescue sex workers, such as prohibitionist feminists and organizations like the Coalition against Trafficking of Women (CATW), one of the biggest anti-trafficking organizations in the United States, whose former executive director I also interviewed.

The polarization between prohibitionist feminists (who want to eliminate prostitution by criminalizing demand) and so-called "sex-positive feminists" (who want to decriminalize all consensual sex between adults, including commercial sex) forms the backdrop of this chapter. My own change of opinion from supporting the Nordic model (a legal model that criminalizes the buying of sex, not the selling of sex) to advocating for decriminalization comes from meeting escorts, hearing their stories, and juxtaposing their views with anti-prostitution activists, who ignore the views or experiences of women like the ones I interviewed.

In this chapter I discuss the absence of sex worker consent from many conceptions of this trade. Why do we believe women lack the agency to consent to be sex workers, on the one hand? And how do we come to view sex workers as unrapeable, on the other? I examine the double bind of consentability and show how damaging it is to the health, safety, and agency of sex workers. I also argue that this ideological double bind has the potential to negatively impact any sexually active woman's ability to consent because it reinforces the separation between good girls and bad girls and encourages the punishment of those considered bad. Therefore, in order to advance the position of women in (and out of) the sex trade, we need to end this polarization.

BIND ONE: PROHIBITIONISM AND THE BELIEF THAT WOMEN CANNOT CONSENT TO SEX WORK

Why do so many people believe women lack the agency to make choices that involve sexual commerce? One answer lies in the deeply rooted and stigmatizing belief that sex work inflicts great harm on women, including degradation (Bindel 2017a; Farley 2004; Jeffreys 1997; Barry 1995, 1979). The idea that someone could choose sex work over working at McDonald's is inconceivable to most anti-prostitution activists, as it was to me at one time. The belief is that whether they realize it or not, sex workers are oppressed because sex work is inherently violent and exploitative. This perspective was articulated to me at length during the making of my film by the former executive director of CATW. Portraying sex work as an exploitative phenomenon that sex workers do not and cannot consent to, she explained:

> We never call anyone a prostitute because prostitution is actually a verb, not a noun; no one is that which is being done to them.... This is the only crime where the crime victim is stigmatized. We don't call other people who have been robbed or raped that which has been done to them, but we do that with prostitution.

When I asked her about the possibility that some women do choose sex work, she answered:

> We understand that prostitution is a function of lack of choice. All of us understand very logically that prostitution is a function of inequality — that it comes out of negative social conditions. And so you have racism, poverty, gender inequality, pimps, you have a whole confluence of forces that push women into prostitution.... [So] if there is someone who says that they are there by choice, well, I might concede 1 percent and then I'll also add to that, besides saying good luck with that, I'll say, ever noticed who's doing the choosing? The people with very few choices.

When I pointed out that all the women I interviewed for my most recent project on sex work had higher education, had worked other jobs and had choice about their work, she suggested that "pro-prostitution" feminists were misguided:

This is nothing but a huge scam being perpetrated by the sex industry to increase their customer base and also much more disturbingly to erase the harm of prostitution. So feminists, some who say they're feminist who accept prostitution, have bought a false bill of goods that somehow this is empowering of women. And I just don't see the logic of that and abolitionists reject that there's any logic to that. Because how is it to be empowered when you are turned into a thing that can be bought and sold by someone with more power than you so there is no, in those feminists, elite feminists' circles that you speak of, that's called agency. And so I just think they've been sold a bill of goods and we need to be, go deeper and think more critically about that.

Knowing that I had thought critically about these issues for some time and had been very much challenged by these women's positive experiences, I persisted. "But what about women who do have options and still prefer sex work?" I asked. "Should we still be criminalizing them and their clients?" Her answer was as follows:

You make social policy [criminalization of the buyers of sex] off of what's happening to [the] 99 percent. You don't make social policy off of the 1 or 2 percent who say it's working well for them. You create social and political legal conditions that foster real meaningful choices that honour the dignity and worth of human beings and do not create vehicles by which people can be used and exploited in this way.

I realized she believed that women should have choices unless they choose sex work. While no doubt well intentioned, setting this limit on women's capacities to consent undermines all women's sexual autonomy, and advocating for the criminalization of sex work increases stigmatization against sex workers. As Lucy argues,

I think the unfortunate part of public perception of sex work is based on two factors, and that's what they see sensationalized either through the trafficking stories and the horrific stories of women or children, you know, being forced to do things against their will or the glamorized sensationalized high-dollar, hottie, high-dollar call girl specials, exposés, or scandals with politicians or, you know, Charlie Sheen or whoever, you know. And those are the spectrums, the bottom end and the high end of it, and there's this huge, I think, area in between that we never see. Part of the reason that we never see it is … because we are quietly and discreetly going about our business without causing any problems in society. We're minding our own business, and we're conducting adult business behind closed doors in the privacy of our own bedrooms, and it's nobody else's business. But beyond that, because of the stigma of it, of course we're also not allowed to talk about it. So even for those of us that have a great working experience and find empowerment and fulfillment through sex work, there's not a lot of opportunities or outlets for us to talk about that publicly with people that are not involved in sex work itself and talk about that honestly.

CATW is not willing to look at mid-range sex workers like Lucy because their experiences don't fit the victim narrative. Prohibitionists consider transactional sex of any kind exploitative, even if the woman selling sex is in a PhD program at a university, is sugar dating for tuition and living expenses, and does not think she's being exploited. Once again, here are the words of the former executive director of CATW:

We've always defined prostitution as including and not limited to just the exchange of money. Trading sex for anything … any time a human being is having sex for any reason other than it's what they want, if they are having sex because they need something, that includes being prostituted.

The women interviewed enjoyed their work and were able to desire sex for money *and* pleasure simultaneously. When I interviewed Lucy after a date with a client and tentatively asked her how it went, and whether it was all about him, she replied, "I think I had 10 or 12 orgasms." In other words, pleasure and money went together for her, as it did for many other women I interviewed. Reinforcing the claim that there was nothing inherently degrading about sex work, Emma stated,

I would say that any woman who wants to do this kind of work ought to be able to do this kind of work. And it runs the gamut of women that have no other skills to women who are highly skilled and have multiple talents and want to do this in addition to the things they can do because they enjoy bringing pleasure to another human being. And as I often say when I'm talking to students, on a scale from one to ten, if murder is the worst thing you can do to your fellow human being, giving them an orgasm has got to be like way up to the top. And I happen to think that giving people pleasure is a good thing, not a bad thing.

CATW's critique of prostitution is, perhaps, applicable to street-based, survival sex workers, but the organization refuses to make the distinction between voluntary and forced prostitution — a distinction made by the United Nations and Amnesty International. Instead, CATW conflates voluntary sex work with involuntary sex trafficking. According to the sex workers I interviewed, the belief that all women who trade sex lack agency is one of the most offensive parts of the anti-prostitution agenda. Emma said,

I mean, why is it an absolute for prostitutes? We're all victims? You know, I mean this is just nonsense because … what it does [claiming all sex workers are victims] is it demeans us by insinuating that we're too stupid to know what we're doing … because they're just patting us on the head and saying, "Oh you poor little stupid girl, you know you don't know any better but you're being exploited by these evil bad men."

But what are the broader consequences of saying that women cannot choose to work as sex workers? Inadvertently or not, anti-prostitution activists increase the stigma for those who do choose sex work. Anti-prostitution groups are clear they want to maintain the stigma of sex work and to increase the stigmatization of male clients to discourage demand. For example, CATW has released a brief outlining its problems with the 2016 Amnesty International policy that calls for the decriminalization of prostitution to protect sex workers and destigmatize sex work. The brief claims that sex work *should* be stigmatized because sex is special and "should be treated differently from other activities" (CATW 2015). Commercial sex, in the organization's words, "trivializes sex." The former executive director of CATW stated it very clearly: "I don't believe that human sexuality is work. I don't believe that every aspect of being a human being can be reduced to labour, to work. I think human sexuality is that part of ourselves, that part of being human that should not be for sale, should not be turned into a commodity that can be bought or sold." Surely this is a moral argument about one's personal view of sexuality, not one that can or should be applied to all people through coercive social policy. Emma said,

> I understand people have a moral issue with prostitution, they have a moral issue with homosexuality and all that. You know what, it isn't their business, and as long as nobody forces them to hire prostitutes or to be a prostitute or to be gay or to engage in a relationship, it just isn't their business to get involved in somebody else's life.

I argue that continuing to approve or disapprove of certain sexualities between consenting adults reinforces rape culture, as it does homophobia and whorephobia (the hatred and abuse of whores and women who are perceived as whores). Stigmatizing women based on their sexual status as good or bad girls is the actual basis of rape culture; some women (the good girls) are to be respected, and some women (the bad girls) are not. As many studies have shown, people feel they have licence to treat those labelled "bad girls" poorly (Benoit et al. 2017; O'Connor 2017; Pauw and Brener 2003). The maintenance of the sexual double standard whereby women but not men acquire stigma through their heterosexual activity encourages women's sexual self-policing, legitimizes sexual violence against women seen as sexually impure, and underlies victim-blaming narratives (Valenti 2009). This double standard is also continuous with whorephobia. So no good comes from continuing to disparage and stigmatize women who choose to be sex workers. CATW supports women whom they consider prostituted but shows no respect for women who choose to be sex workers on the assumption that the latter group can only be deluded or bankrolled by pimps (Bindel 2017b).

BIND TWO: MISOGYNY AND THE BELIEF
THAT SEX WORKERS CANNOT WITHHOLD CONSENT

The more damaging half of the double bind for sex workers is the idea that rape is just part of the job, and sex workers cannot refuse sexual activity. They become unrapeable. Rather than seeing rape as the sexualized violence that it is, regardless of whom it happens to, many people outside of sex work, including police officers and members of the media, contribute to whorephobia in society today by dismissing violence against sex workers and blaming sex workers themselves for these incidents.

This second form of dismissal rests on the belief that a client purchases the right to do anything he wishes to a sex worker. In this way, a sex worker cannot *not* consent, and therefore cannot be raped. One columnist at the *Chicago Sun-Times* even stated that to claim sex workers can be raped is to degrade the experience of "real" sexual assault victims — theft of services, maybe, but assault, not a chance, even when the assault is at gunpoint (*Huffington Post* 2015). A tweeted response to the article succinctly expressed this widespread belief: "Rape a whore? Isn't that just shoplifting?" Rape for sex workers, then, is seen as a hazard of the job and not a serious concern. This twisted logic is similar to the notion that men have permanent right of access to their wives' sexual services, a concept that remained enshrined in Canadian law until the early 1980s, when the marital exemption was removed from rape laws. If women cannot refuse sexual activity because they are sex workers, then they are, of course, vulnerable to abuse and assault because clients know they can get away with it.

Serial killers Robert Pickton and Gary Ridgeway targeted sex workers because they knew most people would not miss them or care. In Ridgeway's chilling words: "I wanted to kill as many women I thought were prostitutes as I possibly could.... I picked prostitutes because I thought I could kill as many of them as I wanted without getting caught." The term "high-risk," often heard in police reports about violent crime, is code for prostitute or drug user. This coding allows many members of the public to blame the victim of violence rather than feel empathy or concern. What did she expect going to a strange man's home to have sex for money? What did she think was going to happen?

There are many examples of sex workers' claims of rape and assault being dismissed because of their occupation (Pauw and Brener 2003; Sullivan 2007). Sex work activists have repeatedly called for police to respond to violence against sex workers, but police are not immune to the misogynistic views about women and sex that dominate in society, and so instead they have contributed to the problem (Dewey and St. Germain 2014; Odinokova et al. 2014). Many sex workers, in fact, think the police are more problematic than the clients. As Amanda related, one of the only negative experiences she had as a sex worker was when she was arrested by undercover police — after they had sex with her:

> In the early '90s, two plain-clothes police officers called me and another girl to their hotel room. They had adjoining rooms. I had sex with the first person, and then they said, "Hey you know, you can make an extra couple hundred dollars if you want to switch." So we switched and then we were both arrested afterwards. After they flushed the condoms.... That is illegal. But it happens all the time. You would be shocked to talk — when you talk to people, you'd be shocked by how many people have similar personal stories or know people that this kind of thing has happened to.

The belief that sex workers "ask for it," or that violence is part of the job, dehumanizes these women and contributes to their abuse. But, as sex workers argue, you can only see violence as an inherent part of the job if you believe that sex is inherently violent. Instead, they argue that it is the stigma and criminalization of sex work that makes sex workers more vulnerable to violence. Notably, the violent predators who target sex workers are not interested in exchanging sex for money but in acting out their violence and hatred of women.

The women I interviewed felt dehumanized and unsafe as a consequence of the notion that sex workers cannot withhold consent. They used strategies to avoid violence, such as carefully screening clients and insisting on respect and dignity in their work. In fact, they saw themselves as experts in negotiating consent and as especially skilled at establishing boundaries. As Dr. Laurie Shrage, one of the researchers in the film, noted, "I think that the public has the wrong idea of sex work. First of all, their clients don't have unlimited sexual access to them.... The terms and the kinds of services that their clients get are often carefully negotiated." The sex workers I spoke to understood consent as ongoing and vocal. Everyone, they believed, has the right to say "yes" or "no" to sexual activity. Again, according to Shrage,

> If in fact sex work were decriminalized and then regulated, it might change the way we look at sex workers. They might not be seen as women who are so subordinate to men because of course they wouldn't be working in an illegal profession. So part of the reason the work is so degrading, especially right now to women, is they are essentially working illegally and therefore always susceptible to a criminal status.

STIGMATIZATION OF SEX WORK AND THE BROADER CULTURE OF SLUT SHAMING

The damaging belief that some women are unable to refuse sexual activity extends beyond sex work into the broader social practice of slut shaming. In her book *Girls and Sex*, Peggy Orenstein (2016) argues that, in the view of the young people she interviewed, once a girl has had sex with a boy, she must always consent to sexual activity not only with the boy in question but with other boys as well. A bad girl, or slut, is viewed as having lost her ability to consent and as deserving of punishment. This can lead to disastrous consequences. There have been numerous examples in North America of slut shaming severe enough to lead girls to suicide: Rehtaeh Parsons, Amanda Todd, Felicia Garcia, Audrie Post, and Cherice Moralez being the most publicized examples (Tanenbaum 2015). These girls were ridiculed and humiliated by people they believed to be friends when photos of incidents best understood as sexual assaults were circulated via social media. Slut shaming is rampant in rape culture with its victim-blaming mentality: You went to his house. You were drunk. You were dressed like a slut. What did you think was going to happen? The blame is on the victim, not the rapist, just as it is when sex workers are targeted for sexual assault.

Many people consider sex work degrading because, in our culture, *sex* is seen to be degrading for women (Valenti 2009). Anti-prostitution activists have unintentionally made it worse for women working in the sex trade by claiming that women cannot possibly choose to do something so demeaning. By maintaining the stigma against sex work, these activists increase the stigma against sex workers themselves. It seems logical to expect that a population seen as unworthy and of diminished value, a population that is blamed when victimized, will be disproportionality targeted for violence. In this way, the activity of anti-prostitution activists could inadvertently perpetuate the violence that sex workers experience.

All women, and especially female sex workers, face double binds and double standards of sexuality, but the most damaging for sex workers are twofold: that women can't consent to their own exploitation by choosing to be sex workers, and that as sex workers they lose the ability to withhold consent to any sexual activity once a service has been paid for (i.e., they become unrapeable). This binary is consistent with the broader, dehumanizing perspective that imagines women and girls are victims with no agency or villains who deserve what happens to them; they are good girls or bad. We should think very carefully about maintaining a distinction that has caused such harm to women over the centuries. Both problematic components of this double bind contribute to the unsafe working conditions and stigma already faced by sex workers, while also reinforcing Western society's rape culture. The women I interviewed taught me that the women who choose sex work will only be released from this paradox when sex work (and sexuality) is no longer stigmatized and criminalized.

Chapter 11

WHAT YOU CAN DO, WHAT YOU CAN'T DO, AND WHAT YOU'RE GOING TO PAY ME TO DO IT

A First-Person Account of Survival and Empowerment through Sex Work

Debra Paris Perry

in interview with KelleyAnne Malinen

Debra Paris Perry is a sex work activist and service provider in Halifax, Nova Scotia, who draws on first-person knowledge to support girls and women who have been trafficked, to advocate for decriminalization of sex work, and to challenge stereotypes about those who work in the sex trade. Her nuanced perspective covers some of the ways and reasons women come to sex work voluntarily and consensually, while also recognizing how structural forms of violence, intergenerational trauma, and the law of "supply and demand can push women into this industry." Thus, her narrative complicates what is typically a polarized debate over the question of whether sex work is consensual.

This chapter is a redacted version of some of Debra's story, which was shared in conversation with KelleyAnne Malinen. Debra begins this telling with her great-great-grandparents, who on one side of her family were sold into slavery in Barbados, and on the other were confined to residential schools in Canada. Drawing on this history, her childhood, and her experiences in and observations about sex work, Debra highlights structures, relationships, and intersections between sexism, racism, and anti-indigeneity.

Today, Debra helps deliver two YWCA programs: Safe Landing and NSTEP (Nova Scotia Tracking Elimination Partnership). Through this work, she provides education about sex trafficking and will eventually support women who have been trafficked or who are looking to move from careers in sex work to new occupations.

FAMILY AND COLONIAL HISTORY

Deb: Because of the Underground Railroad coming here, there are a lot of people who are mixed. For one thing, Indigenous People knew that Aboriginal children get taken: They get taken by residential schools, they go through the foster scoop,[1] but if your child could identify as Black, they didn't get stolen. A lot of the dark Indians identified as Black, because at that time the push was "Kill the Indian, save the child."[2] People who are actually Aboriginal became Black — lived in Black communities, married Black people — both men and women, so there's a very large population. Another part of the mixed history is, if you're enslaving Brown people, why go hundreds of miles away to get your Brown people when you already have Brown people right there? A lot of us were enslaved, but we didn't come from Africa. We were dark Indians that could be stamped as Black so we could be slaves.

KA: Can you trace that history in your family?

Deb: With the Parises, with my great-great-grandparents, I can go back as far as Barbados, which is where most of the slave trading happened. That's where most of them were named. Whoever bought them, they used their last name. My Aboriginal family, we're from a reserve in Alberta called Wabasca. It used to be named after the priest who ran the school, and the Native people renamed it and reclaimed it as Wabasca, and that's where my great-grandmother was and my great-great-grandmother. My mom was working in Manitoba and my dad met her as a porter on the train.

KA: There were a lot of Black porters.

Deb: That was *the* job to have. You were a butler on the train. I used to go on the train with my father, and they made beds, they did the cleaning. People would set their shoes outside their rooms, and the porters would come shine the shoes and then put them back. But the food was good, they got a salary, they got to travel, and they also could sometimes bring their families on trips, which is probably something that wouldn't have been afforded to them otherwise, right?

All the other workers knew, Clyde's daughter is on the train. I was very young, so they would keep an eye on me as they went. At nighttime, any berth that wasn't already rented to someone, I could have. So I spent from the age of five to the age of nine on the trains.

KA: You have good memories of that?

Deb: Well I do, I do. The bad memories are kind of over there. You know? I'm very good at that, I just — I'm very good at cherry-picking my memories now. But yeah, I remember sitting back in the fancy dining room and eating good. I was in the back part of the dining room of course, but I was still there.

You know, I didn't start school until I was around seven, because my father had stoled me, so he couldn't register me in school. What happened is my mom ended up in the hospital. She had a miscarriage because of my father beating her. The baby was stillborn. My mom continued to think that she was pregnant, so of course they put her in the hospital. There was a big story about this judge who had her committed. He got in all kinds of trouble because he was beating his own wife and stuff. He was giving custody to the fathers all the time and finding the mothers unfit. She ended up at that time in the Victoria General [in Halifax], 9A for psychiatric, and we all ended up in the Colored Home.[3] Reverend Fairfax came for us. He was infamous for taking children to the home and for abusing children himself. Later, I ended up with my grandmother in Truro, and my brother ended up just up here at 2468 Creighton with my uncle. My sister was given to my aunt and uncle in New Glasgow, because she [the aunt] couldn't have any more children and she only had boys and wanted a girl. Those are my mother's children. She's the one that has the most children from my father. There's seventeen moms, with twenty-one children, but anyway.

KA: Do you all know each other?

Deb: Yup. I'm the oldest of my father's children, so I made it a point to know them, the reason being that I spent a lot of years not fitting in within the Aboriginal community or the Black community. The Black girls would say, "Oh, you think because you're high yellow and you've got good hair that you're better than me." And I never thought that, but that was their own ghosts, right?

And then within the Aboriginal community I was a slap me five Indian,[4] because I had a behind and I had a full mouth, and that was something that Native people don't have. They were taught lighter was better.

I think I was nine when I re-met my mom, and I was always really angry with her, because — what can I say? — there was abuse and stuff in my family. People didn't acknowledge it as abuse. It was little girls and boys playing. I don't know how to even explain it. The sickness was intergenerational.

KA: So like, sexual abuse?

Deb: Yeah, yeah. My grandmother would say, "Don't go pickin' blueberries by yourself, because if you do the boys will get you and it will be your fault." They never told the boys, "Keep your fuckin' hands to yourself." We didn't have to go to the outhouse, because of safety issues, so we had the pot in the house. We were always told to stay in little girl groups, because if anything did happen — you know?

KA: That sounds very familiar.

Deb: Yeah, yeah. I don't think that was by colour or culture — or I think it was cultural but across the board. If you are a victim of violence, it's your fault. You know, 'cause these guys can't help themselves, and we are supposed to acknowledge that, and know it, and make excuses for them all the time.

I've always been considered Clyde's crazy daughter because I've spoken out about abuse. I think I became that kid when I realized, "This is not normal!" This does not happen in everybody's home. This is not what fathers expect from their daughters or what cousins expect from their female cousins. I mean, I can't say it didn't feel okay at the time, because it's what I knew, but once I realized that this is not what the expectation of girls should be....

I think I really realized when my cousin was finally moving out. She said, "I really feel bad about leaving you here by yourself." She said, "You take care of yourself, it's only a few more years, and then you'll be able to get out of here too." So, you kind of dealt with it. You learned not to fight things because fighting only made it worse.

Growing up in residential school, mom said nothing actually happened to her, but she saw it happen to other people. I don't know how true that is, but I think that's her truth for now. Anyway, she didn't consider that she was being abused by having to watch that being done to someone else. When they opened up Adam's Paradise [massage parlour], which was one of the first ones, she said, "They got this place, and they only do hand jobs there." She didn't think that was such a terrible thing. Right? And neither did I, just with my history. So, you gotta jerk them off — no big deal. Although I would always be jerking and gagging at the same time. My sister and I laugh, because we both ended up in the sex trade, although neither one of us can stand the smell of semen and both of us are scared of the dark [laughs].

KA: So when you think about the path that brought you to sex work —

Deb: I want to tell you this: Every sex worker's story can be just as individual as the woman or man who tells them. Some of us do come from abusive families. Some of us don't.

But yeah, it was poverty, it was necessity, but I also think it became normal because I knew that if I sat on Uncle Joe's lap, he would give me a quarter, and if I sat on Uncle Bill's lap, he would give me a dollar. Right? So I learned that.

Later when I started speaking out about things that weren't okay, of course my family wanted to ostracize me because they didn't want that stuff being public, but I didn't care. I didn't care. I was self-medicating, so I would come home for a visit and people would say [whispers], "Oh, that's Clyde's crazy daughter. You know, the one who does drugs and stuff," right? They invalidated my stories, to the point where I started to wonder, "Did it happen to me?"

I've always used humour to fight through my pain, and people that know me know I still do that today. I'd be at a family reunion, and one of my uncles would say, "I remember when I used to change your diapers."

I would say, "And I remember when I wasn't in diapers anymore and you were still trying to get in my pants" [laughs]. And the room would go silent. I can tell you that I had to find out when things were going on and just show up, 'cause nobody was inviting me. I wanted everyone to know what they'd done.

KA: But you still wanted to be at the family events.

Deb: Well, because that's my family! I was very close to my family and my uncles and stuff. I learned to separate who they were from what they did.

I got married to a guy who was so much like my father, and he would beat me up five days a week, but I lived for the [other] two days, and I made excuses for him, right? The guy works all day, and he should come home and have a hot meal on the table. I worked all day too, so I would have to get off work and then get home and get the meals ready and maybe the potatoes had lumps in them. So as a good wife, I should know how to make non-lumpy potatoes. So, learning how to make excuses for him, and live for the two days a week when he wasn't beating my head in.

When I started fighting back, physically fighting back, he was in *shock*. He stood there and he said, "You hit me!" I said, "You hit me first!" I just decided, *I am not doing this anymore.*

One of my sons can be aggressive towards women. The other one is aggressive towards men who are aggressive towards women, okay? When one of my many daughters-in-law came to me — and I call them daughters-in-law even though they weren't married to my sons because I hate people being called the "baby mama" — she called and she said that he hit her and she didn't know what to do. I said, "I'll tell you what to do: You go get a truck, and take everything you want, and on your way out of town, call the police and charge his ass. That's what you do."

She said, "You're not going to be mad at me if I do that?"

Why would I be? I remembered my sisters-in-law being mad at me because the neighbour called the police and my husband got charged and I went to court. I remember my sisters-in-wanting to beat me up, because they were in the same mindset where I was at one time: "Well what did *you* do?"

VIOLENCE AGAINST SEX WORKERS

Deb: I rallied in Parade Square a few years ago when they did a proc-lamation[5] for the Day to End Violence Against Sex Workers, and I was crying. I had already been in the business for about thirty years off and on. I just couldn't believe that people would make a proclamation like that.

I think [Halifax mayor] Mike Savage was supposed to read it, but he didn't show up. The mayor in Dartmouth, [Gloria] Mc-Cluskey, had to read it, and I remember how against the sex work-ers she was. She's very much an abolitionist, right? I remember looking at her choking on the words [laughs]. She started things like this committee of people in the neighbourhood to take peo-ple's licence plates and to chase the girls around with signs.[6]

It was like the time [Nova Scotia medical examiner] Roland Perry put pictures of that girl on the news about her being HIV positive and if you had sex with her then you'd better get to the doctor. Suddenly everybody thought all sex workers had AIDS, and that became another reason for people to be violent towards us. There was me trying to explain, "Listen, if you drive a cab, you take care of your car, okay?" Simple.

We've already got the moral majority and the police after us. And then we've got the psychos because we are made non-people as sex workers, you know? That's how the press shows us. We've got people that are trying to hurt us, and people who say that is a complication of your job. The last thing that you want to do is get infected, because if you did pass that on, then you've got someone else trying to kill you. You try to lessen the [number of] people trying to kill you [laughs].

We tried to make a bad date list with the description of the guy, the car, the licence plate, but the police wanted to go after all the tricks. They thought they were making us more safe, but they were making our job even more unsafe.

I was attacked by a customer once. I could see it coming, because I could see the way he was driving. I grew up in an alcoholic home, so you learn to notice signs. You learn how to walk on eggshells and not to make too much noise in the morning, because there's hangovers. I *learned* not to have lumps in my potatoes, so that my husband didn't have the right to beat me up. When you're in sex work, you learn a lot of those things.

People don't drive with two hands on the steering wheel like this anymore. It's usually one handed, and they're kind of laid-back, so when you see someone white-knuckle driving, you know something's going on. I said to buddy, "You know what? After thinking about it, I think maybe I should just go, because I think you might be happier with somebody else."

He pulled a knife, and he said, "You're gonna suck my dick, and I'm gonna cum down your throat."

I said, "The only way you're cumming down my throat is if you cut my head off." It just wasn't going to happen. I grabbed the knife by the blade, and I held onto it, and I said to him, "If you're crazy enough to cut my throat, then you're crazy enough to cut my fingers off to do it, because I'm not letting go of this knife." It had a wooden handle. It was one of these long fish-filleting knives. I knew, because I worked at Forty Fathoms fish plant.

Then he said, "Okay, you proved yourself. You're a macho. Get out of my truck."

I said, "No, if you're gonna kill me, you're gonna kill me in your truck, so my blood and shit will be all over, so people will find out it was you." I'm having this conversation the whole time holding onto the knife, with blood streaming down my arm. I thought, "This guy's talking too much, he's not going to kill me." If someone's gonna kill ya, they're going to kill ya. They're not going to say anything.

He knew where we were going, so I could tell he had done this before. A couple of women that were sex workers confirmed that later. Another thing I learned growing up in an alcoholic home, I learned to scan rooms and find what I could use to defend myself. I scanned, and I saw a hole in the fence. He had driven into this parking lot and parked so on my side was a long metal light pole, so I couldn't open the door, right? For a minute I started to freak out, but then I realized, "Deb, you need to pull it together. You need to deal with this" [snaps fingers]. He told me to get out, and I said "No, you're not killing me in the parking lot. If you kill me it's going to be in your truck. You get out, and when you get out, go way over there, then I'll get out. Otherwise, I'm staying here." So, he got out of his driver's side, then I had to get out the driver's side, because my side was pressed against the pole. Then I knew to run around the front of the truck, and there's a hole right there.

I went through the hole in this metal fence, tore my arm all up, and then he jumped in the truck and came after me and tried to run me over. I saw this other guy with his door open, a garbage bag in each hand, and I ran past him right into his house. When I ran in, his woman was there, and she started screaming. I said, "Please call the police. Somebody's trying to kill me." My hand was bleeding, my arm was bleeding, my clothes were ripped.

The police showed up and they said, "Oh. It's you." I was very much known to the police as a sex worker. This cop was like, "What do you want me to do about this? Most of you girls don't even show up at court."

I said, "I want you to do your job." I was just tired. I was tired of allowing rapes to happen to me and not go to the police. I was tired of the abuse that happened to me. You guys are supposed to be protecting people! Do your frigging job. I don't care what my job is. Your job is *this*!

I said to him, "Listen. Here's the way it is, okay? You have five days to get this guy. I'm describing the truck and the licence plate and the person, right down to the little scar under his eye and the buckles of his motorcycle boots. There's no reason why you cannot get this guy. If I don't hear from you in five days, I'm going to every rainbow organization that I belong to, I'm going to every sex worker thing, I'm going to every woman's organization, I'm going to every Black and Aboriginal organization — they are going to be on your ass 'cause you did not do your job. I'm sick of it and tired of it."

And they said, "Well, you know your name's gonna get in the paper and everybody will know what you do." I said, "Everybody including you already know what I do." I don't care at this point.

When buddy got the paper with my name on it from the court, he went through the phonebook and started calling people.

My cousin told me, "Some freaky guy called looking for Debbie."

He finally reached my mom, who is quite old, and was like, "May I please speak with Debra?"

"She's not here right now, can I —"

"Well you just give her a message for me, and tell her if she shows up for court, it won't be healthy for her or you."

I call the police. I tell them what happened.

They say, "Have you ever talked to this guy on the phone?"

I say, "No."

"Has your mother?"

"No."

"Well then how do you know it was him?"

Come on! I mean, by process of deduction? I'm not going to court against anyone else right now.

"Well we can't prove it was him, so it doesn't even make sense to make a report on this" is what they said to me.

I did go to court. The guy opted for Supreme Court, because he wanted judge and jury. I knew that he was going to get off because he owned a very large business in Bedford. Joel Pink was his lawyer. Joel always has people who come in first, and he comes in later. He had his first chairs and all that crap, then I remember seeing him flying in in his court gear.

They start asking me ridiculous questions: "If he had a Coke can, and then he was driving, how do you know it wasn't the Coke can that was the silver you saw? Maybe you cut your hand on the Coke can."

So now I'm starting to get agitated. I look over at the jury. Of course, it was all white and all very "pinched-nosed women," I call them, because they always look like there's a little turd of shit under their nose, and they're all Margaret Thatcher looking. I knew that *I* was already convicted. I was not the victim.

But I told my story anyway. I mean, he tried to lie. He said, "Oh, I was at a stop sign and she jumped into my truck."

I said, "Your Honour, do you have pictures of his truck in front of you? It has stairs. That night, I had a little black leather mini-skirt that I had to pull up around my waist to step up into his truck. How could I have pulled his truck door open and jumped in at a stop sign?"

Of course, he was found not guilty. As I'm leaving the court, I remember his wife sitting there. I turned to her first, and I said, "If this is what he would do to me, I know that he's beating you at home. And the fact that you could listen to this stuff and support him also means that he's doing it to you too, and I feel bad for you, and I hope someone helps you."

And then I turned to him: "And for you, this is one twenty-thousand-dollar blow job that you never got." Because I know Joel don't walk into a courtroom for less than twenty grand. "So, next time, just pay the fucking money. Okay buddy?"

And then I get back to the YW — so this is an all-female residence — and there's notes under the door from other women saying that they don't want me there because I'm a hooker and they don't feel safe. They cut stuff out of the paper, put that under the office door, trying to get me put out. Wanda [YWCA staff] didn't though. She didn't put me out. No, the staff didn't. Wanda's still there, and we laugh about that now.

ENLIGHTENED

KA: What did you actually need at that time?

Deb: I needed someone that would separate me from what I do as a living. I was a woman. I was like any other woman that had been attacked and abused. Even in places for women, we're still "those girls," right? We're still "those girls." At one point I got sent to a place in New Brunswick, and the girl said, "You don't fit our mandate." Why? 'Cause I'm not sitting in the corner crying all the time? They told me to get out or they were going to call the police.

I said, "You know what, I'm really happy that I'm in a strong place." If I had not been strong that day, or if I had been in my broken stage — my victim stage — as opposed to my victor and my warrior, I could have just gone out that night and laid down in the snow and went to sleep thinking "nobody cares about me." I said, "I'm going to call Victim Services, because right now you guys are revictimizing me, and I need some help." Victim Services in Cape Breton put me in this little apartment hotel, and they paid for it until social services would. They were really, really great. It was about finding people that could separate me from my job. That was my *job*.

Over the years, a lot of my friends have been murdered, or have killed themselves, or have died of overdose, and a lot of it is because of how sex workers are seen and treated. One woman that I knew who was murdered and dabbled a little bit in addictions and maybe had to do a few things to supply her habit — we couldn't even go and mourn at her funeral because the media didn't know that she had been involved in drugs or the sex trade. If they had, the police wouldn't have bothered to find her murderer. People have an idea that people in the sex trade don't care about anything, and we're stupid, and the only job we know how to do is to lay on our backs. I hear those things all the time.

I did a presentation at Mount Saint Vincent University a long time ago. At that time, our radical lesbian feminist groups were giving me the hardest times about my choices. A few of the women had said to me that "you aren't *enlightened*, and that's why you feel that swinging on a pole is okay or hooking is okay." I was at the Mount for this presentation, and I remember walking around with a book on my head being sarcastic and also so people would ask me why.

So, people were saying, "Why do you have this book on your head, Deb?"

I said, "'Cause I am afraid I might get enlightened here at the Mount. I'm not quite sure what that is, but it sounds like it would hurt." All I could think of was lightning striking me, enlightening me. They laughed and laughed. Like I said, I use humour so I can do it, but it was also my way of saying, "This is so stupid," right?

You guys gotta remember that I'm older than a lot of you. I was there when women were burning their bras, and we were there to support each other in *choice*. We ousted the testicles, and then the radical lesbian feminists — I didn't label them, that's who they decided to call themselves! — they came in and decided if I want to stay home and bake cookies, I'm not fulfilling myself. If I want to work on a pole, I'm not enlightened. If I want to run a jackhammer, *then* I'm enlightened. So now we've ousted the testicles, and we've brought in these people who are still trying to tell us what our choices should be.

IT'S A BUSINESS

KA: Are there plus sides to being a sex worker?

Deb: There are. In my situation, coming up the way I did, the first time that I could say to a man "This is what you can do, this is what you can't do, and this is what you're going to pay me to do it" was very empowering to me. Someone who has not experienced what I've experienced might not get it, but it put me in control of my body.

I've had clients say to me, "Well, are you a hooker or not?"

"I am, but not with you today." The same as when they went through the abortion thing: my body, my choice.

Plus, I had money! I wasn't in a situation where I had to depend on somebody else for stuff. I made a thousand bucks a day, because as you see by the interview, I've got the gift of gab. When I worked for the escort service, it was an hourly rate. I would talk for fifty-five minutes about anything — the gestation period of the sperm whale — anything! And then I would look at him: "Oh my god! We've only got five minutes left." And no guy is going to admit that he can get off in five minutes, so I'd say, "Well, we either gotta do it right now and get it done, or you gotta take another hour."

When I turned out, I turned out with girls. I was thirteen, and it was out of necessity because I was on the run from the Nova Scotia School for Girls in Truro, which is the girl equivalent of Shelbourne, so everybody knows those horror stories.[7] I needed to live, I needed to eat, I couldn't get a job — I was thirteen.

I was sitting down in Dominion Square, panhandling, and one of the girls said, "You know what? You can do better than this." I looked at her as a woman. She was sixteen, but she had been in the trade for three years already. She gave me a $20 bill in my cup. It still would be a lot if you put $20 in somebody's cup on Spring Garden Road today, right? And she gave me a phone number. She said, "If you wanna do something different, get a hold of me."

I remember my first customer. He was a jockey from Blue Bonnets Raceway in Montreal, and I remember it because I thought I had to stay there until he was done. That's what I was used to, right? Letting people get done. They came and knocked on the door: "Up some more money, bud. If you're gonna stay there, you gotta give more money." Then I started realizing, "Hey! I don't have to just let people — I can get paid for this."

There was a pimp around somewhere, but I never saw him. I know they made money off me, and that's fine. You pay for your education when you go to college, so I'm not mad about it. I paid for my education.

Often guys that are turning you out will just be like, "There's where you get 'em, there's where you take 'em, and I'll be back." Women will teach you how to take care of yourself. They'll teach you how to look for crabs and things. And you would be surprised how many guys will offer you extra not to use a condom. These women told me, "Always remember hooking is what you do, not who you are. It's a job." And I think that was a saving grace for me.

The girls I worked with at that time knew what would sell. They told me, "Put pigtails in your hair." My work uniform was a pair of baby doll pajamas with frills on the bum. Now when you look back at it, that's really fuckin' sick, right? I didn't know I was feeding a sickness of people. It made me a lot of money though. We need to start looking more at why a man of 45 or 50 would want to have sex with a child that's young enough to be his grandkid, and what happens in society to make that okay.

The sex trade is supply and demand. It's a business! As long as that's what the white men want, then that business is gonna be there. When exotic women were in, boy I made money, 'cause I could be all kinds of different things just because of my skin colour and hair texture. "Oh, you want a Spanish girl? *Mira! Papi!*" I could be all those things. But when the supply and demand became young, white girls....

When big conventions and stuff come here, we know what they're gonna be looking for. They usually only take one Black girl, 'cause even the guys that want Black girls don't want other white guys to know that they want a Black girl. I used to run a massage parlour and it was like [whispers], "I'll come back later. Save the Black one for me," because they didn't want their friends to know. So even the escort services will only take one Black girl. When you knew that a convention was in town, you wanted to get there quickly to be that first Black girl. I could pass for Spanish, so I could get in some places where darker-skinned Black women might not have. Plus, living in New York I learned a little Spanish.

When the cruise ships come in, they have these entertainment people, and they will take a busload of guys and go hunting for girls. The guys will go to the cab drivers and say, "Listen, I'm only here for three hours. Can you get me a girl?" Stuff like that. And the demand usually is for young, white girls, because the men feel they're less used or something. I don't know.

KA: Yes, then on the flip side, Indigenous women and Black women talk about how never having given a thought to doing sex work, they can be going about their business and get propositioned, and how that is harmful.

Deb: Yes, yes. When really, the population of Black and Indigenous women in the whole of the sex trade is small. People will come into my neighbourhood though and solicit faster than they would on Spring Garden Road, because they know poverty's here, so the chances of getting a "yes" are better, or because people in our neighbourhood don't deal with the cops. If I approach this white girl, she might be a cop trying to bust me. But I know that the Black girls aren't police, right? They think it's our cultural norm. If women of colour don't speak out about trafficking, they think we agree with it. In fact, we just worry about our safety, because the police don't worry about it.

TRICKS

KA: Do you think the tricks love their wives?
Deb: Yep. Sex, love — some people understand the separation, and

I honestly think most of my clients love their wives. I know that sounds crazy to a lot of people, but they're being respectful. It's a business transaction. Everybody knows where they stand in this transaction: They're not gonna show up at your door, because it's not an affair. I was married to a guy in the navy, and I said to him, "I know your sexual appetite when you're home, so I don't know if that lessens when you're away. Pay for it, use protection, and it's not supper conversation. I can deal with that. But for a woman to show up because you lied to her, or you got a baby now on the way, that would be devastating to me."

I worked at an escort service where one wife would bring her husband 'cause he was into domination, and she'd say, "I used to beat him, but I can't beat him anymore, so bring him here for you girls to beat him." I had moms who would call me because they had sons with disabilities but still were sexual, and the moms wanted their sons to experience that, but in the real world it was much harder for them to get laid.

I have clients that became friends after a while. I remember saying to one that I'd been seeing for twenty-something years as a client, "I've been through two weddings with you, two bachelor parties, two divorces, and now you're on your third marriage." And he said, "Yeah, and at the end of the day Deb, you've cost me less than any of them" [laughs]. Because we have an understanding about where things are, and what it's about.

Now the psycho guys — they're different. They just hate all women. They hate their wives, and they can't beat their wives up because they don't want to go to jail, so they'll beat up a hooker that no one's gonna care about.

KA: How does the ideal trick act?

Deb: First off, he knows what's up. He knows this is a business transaction. I've had clients say, "I'll leave my wife." For what? Where are you going? Because you're definitely not coming here. The only reason you want me to be your girlfriend is because you want to get what you've been paying for for nothing. I'm not stupid. And then you'll pay for someone else, because you've got an addiction, which is hookers. Most of the people that we see get laid. They don't *have* to come to us.

But the ideal trick is respectful. He talks to you like anyone else. He knows that just because it's an hour doesn't mean you get to pick at me for an hour, right? I don't want to be picked at for an hour. And of course, non-violent — unless that's something that you two have agreed upon, 'cause some women are okay with that. I'm not. It kinda brings back old ghosts, so I can't.

A BOUNDARY WHERE MY HEART IS

Deb: I did a lot of time in the domination room though, because of my stature and my heavy voice. I had to stop because I got to like it too much.

KA: Why was that not okay?

Deb: It wasn't okay because I felt that I could really maybe hurt somebody. In order to get my head in that space, I had to think about people that had abused me or hurt me. I don't even kill bugs, you understand? I walk around and I pick up worms when it rains and I put them back in the grass 'cause I know we need the worms to aerate the soil or we're all gonna die. So that's my heart. I catch hornets while everyone else is freaking out and swatting at them. I tell them, "Buddy, you gotta leave," because that's my heart. But when I sat down and thought about some of the people who had abused me, it was easy for me to reciprocate that violence. That's not who I am, and I didn't want to be that person.

For other girls — no problem. The stigma is all about what's the flavour of the week for the moral majority. People thought *Fifty Shades of Grey* was wonderful! But if we had brought that in? [laughs] That woman from Toronto was charged with sex charges for being a dominatrix.[8] She took a lot of flak. But someone writes *Fifty Shades of Grey*, and now everyone wants to be tied up. It's whatever the flavour happens to be.

PIMPING

KA: What's your feeling on pimping?

Deb: Well, okay. I am 100 percent against anybody forcing anybody to do anything they don't want to do. But I am also 100 percent for choices that people make. I think that people don't understand it.

For example, I was in a family of twelve. I was happy to be there. I wasn't forced. It was the family that I never had 'cause we did what families are supposed to do, which is take care of each other and watch each other's back, and make sure that everybody had what they needed.

I'm not super sexual, and that has nothing to do with my job, it has to do with my life. I want more than just sex. When I lay down with someone because I want to, there has to be emotions attached, and having sex with the lights on with your eyes open so you know that it's me and that I'm not just anybody. Finding a lover that learns what I want and what I need — that can only happen through time. Some of the other girls would get jealous about our man sleeping with the other girls. I was like, "If he don't come bother me for two weeks, I'm happy." For me it was about the family.

A lot of the times it's not the guy, it's the girl who says, "I wanna work, and I want you to come with me to Toronto." Now, I'm not saying that people aren't forced. I've seen it happen where girls are taken to Toronto in a trunk, but that's more rare. One reason that the girls come home as victims is because you guys shame them, and by "you guys," I mean general society. If I come home and say, "Oh, he forced me to do it and I didn't want to" — which again is sometimes the case — I will get help. If it's like, "Well I tried it, man, wasn't my thing," then I get revictimized and shamed. Women shouldn't have to be victims to get what they need.

After I'd been in the sex trade for a while, my male partner stayed home. I had a house husband, which would probably be considered legally a pimp, but he wasn't. I just knew I could make five times the money he made in less time, and I was okay with what I was doing.

Lucky for me, I only ever had a real pimp once, and that was because everyone had one. It was like having a dog in your purse [laughs], so I thought, "Okay, I'll try this." I worked for a little bit, and then I thought, "I'm not giving you all my fucking money!" I mean, I'm not.

The other girls said, "If you get caught stashing, he'll beat ya."

I'm like, "Stashing what? My own fucking money? Why?"

They said, "Protection."

I'm like, "But he's not in the backseat with me. He's not in the hotel room with me. He's out partying somewhere, and I'm getting killed. So how is that protecting me?" I just could never get my head around it.

When I told him I was going to leave, of course he got mad, because I was always a money maker. I went to boosting school, so I wasn't just a hooker, I was a big-time shoplifter. They do have schools by the way, where you actually learn how to boost.

KA: That's interesting.

Deb: I know. It's a totally different culture.

I remember it was winter time, because I had just bought a bunch of stuff for my kids and a really nice pot set for my mom. He knew I was going home for the holidays, and I told him I wasn't coming back. I said, "This isn't for me. I'm not happy." Then I laid down waiting for the airport people to pick me up for the next day, but when I woke up I was duct taped. Yup.

He beat me really, really badly, and he said, "You're not going home for the holidays. You're going to work."

I said, "Yeah, okay." But I knew, as soon as I get out on the street, I'm gone, buddy. Right? So off I went. I waited till I knew that he was out, I snuck back to the hotel, I got the gifts, and I took off. I went home.

THE BLACK/WHITE MYTH

Deb: In my work with the Anti-Trafficking Strategy, I'm trying to get rid of this Black/white myth where, you know, pimps are all Black and victims are all white. I'm trying to get away from that, which is what society has given. You have to make it so it works for the powers that be, like it's for their benefit [laughs]. For example, when I was trying to set up a needle exchange, and I went to the medical professionals, I had to frame it like, "Wouldn't *you* rather deal with someone who's been using clean needles?" So, for Anti-Trafficking, we talk about, "You're hurting yourselves and you're hurting your children by only giving the pimp one look."

I ran The Aristocrat, which was on King Street. There was Adam's Paradise down here, and Cousin Brucie's. I remember people calling Ada McCallum an *icon*.[9] The newspapers glorified her.[10] They vilify everyone else. Ada was a pimp. Just because she was an older white lady doesn't make that okay. It makes life easy for people like the lawyer that just got busted for pimping,[11] or for the gamer-looking guy that now has seventy-four charges, when everyone believes and tells their children that pimps are big Black guys from North Preston.

We teach about what the grooming process looks like, where the guy tells you, "Oh, you're my girlfriend, and we just have to do this for a little while." I'm not saying that isn't true sometimes, but it's also part of the process. And they know who to approach. Their job as procurers is to find people that they can coerce. They are as versed in their work as we are in ours. They're called the "gentleman pimps." They'll find a girl that they know needs a daddy. I couldn't imagine having sex with someone I called daddy. That would be gross to me, but these young women will do that — "That's my daddy!"

We also talk about how a lot of the girls are going to work on their own now. Why is that? We all know women are lower paid, finding jobs can be more difficult, and then if you have children, childcare can cost more than work will pay. So all of those things.

People say to me all the time, "What if your daughter had decided to do that work?" What's so funny is my daughter's a cop, but I say, "Well, first I'd want to show her all the different options out there. But if that's still something she wanted to do, I would tell her to get the proper education and learn to do it safely." I couldn't be the one to mentor her in that, because she's still my kid.

CHOICE IN REALITY

KA: So, in all of that, how do you think about choice? The difference between choice and force is really important, clearly. Where is the distinction between the two?

Deb: When I was younger, it was necessity. Necessity isn't quite the same as force, but you know, I should have had more options. I made the best choice for me at the time. Also, it was what I knew. I shouldn't have had to have known that. In a normal world, or in a wonderful world, I wouldn't have already had some of the skills that it took.

Choice for me became later on. I'm a CCA [continuing care assistant], I'm a holistic veterinary assistant, I've held a variety of jobs, but still the only reason that I'm not hooking is because my hooking and addictions became so hand in hand that I could make $1,000 a day but I was spending $995 on drugs. It was just the routine, and the fact that the money made that degree of drug use possible. I wasn't using to cope with the work.

KA: So what are some things that need to change?

Deb: Just start talking to hookers. We're not dragons, we're not monsters, we're not gonna cut your throat, we're not gonna steal your money. Stop telling us what we need, and ask what we need. That's the best way to know.

Sex work's always gonna be here, so for everybody to do whatever they do safely is what's really important. I think decriminalization is our first step. I'm talking about adults. I think kids under nineteen should be given other opportunities. I don't really know how many of them are mature enough to make such life-changing choices, although if they do make those choices they should be supported and kept safe.

When I look back now — because people say, "Would you change things?" — I'll never know that, because I made the best choice for me out of the limited choices that I had. I think it needs to be about opening up *more* choices. Also, I think community shaming needs to be gone. Once it's decriminalized, people won't be able to shame you for being a hooker, because it's a job.

Like I said, I went back to school — I'm educated — but in none of those other jobs would I make money like in the sex trade. I'm my own boss. I work when I want to. But that doesn't mean if they decriminalize it, everyone's gonna do it. I remember trying to get condoms in schools years ago, and they were like, "Oh no, you can't give them condoms, they're going to have sex." Well, they're already having sex. Look at all the unplanned pregnancies!

We tried to get condoms and needles into the jails. That was another project that I worked on, and they're like, "No."

We're like, "So you're saying there's no sex in jail?" You're not taking into consideration that people are gay before going to jail, so it's not always some kinda jailhouse rape [laughs]. You're not taking into consideration that people go in with addictions and don't get the proper support, so they're still using. The guards see the money-making opportunity, so they're bringing most of the drugs in. People just don't want to look at the reality of things, because once you see reality, you gotta deal with it.

So that's where decriminalization comes in. Although I worry that once it's decriminalized, social services will do your community assessment for work, and your community services worker will say, "Your score says hooker! You go hook!" [laughs] Is that okay? I don't know. I don't think that works either.

Chapter 12

TENDER PLACES

On the Intersection of Anti-Rape Activism and Prison Abolitionism

El Jones and Ardath Whynacht — A Dialogue

This chapter is a conversation about the relationship between two political commitments we share: anti-rape activism and prison abolitionism. Our dialogue is partially motivated by encounters each of us have had with people who do not believe one can simultaneously take a strong position against rape and advocate against incarceration. The apparent belief is that anti-rape activism requires demanding long sentences for perpetrators of sexual violence. On the contrary, we see incarceration as continuous with rape culture. Indeed, prison abolitionism could well be considered a mode of anti-rape activism. What follows is a transcription of our oral exchange.

FINDING A PATH

El: Ardath, you and I have known each other for a decade through spoken word and then different sites of activism and academic work. And actually, the first time I went to a woman's prison was when you were doing creative writing at the women's federal prison and you asked me to come in. And I always remember driving back with you, and you were thinking that maybe you should have told me what the women had been convicted of in case it bothered me, and we had a conversation about how really it didn't seem to matter in that space. And you said something that's always stuck with me: "I wish I could find the same forgiveness for people in my own life that I find in there." I think about that quite often, because I think it really honestly encapsulates this struggle we have between how we think theoretically about abolition and then how we actually put that into practice.

And I feel like that's one starting point for this conversation — how do we find a path through a commitment to prison abolition, on the one hand, and the current feminist discourse around rape culture, which often relies upon incarceration of a measure of how seriously society takes sexual assault? And how do we do this in a way that realistically respects the anger we have, the real desire for vengeance we feel when we've been wronged, and how we actually live out the ways we've been wronged in our own lives?

Ardath: That's always been my struggle in doing prison abolition work and anti-violence work in the community. We are always, already, implicated in the prison state. We are socialized from the moment we are born to seeing punishment as a solution to harm. It's complex. I have a tremendous amount of empathy for folks in prison who have done terrible things.... I teach and write poems with men who have murdered and sexually assaulted women, and I have developed friendships with them over time. But at the same time, if someone were to harm my family in those same ways, the proximity of the harm would compromise my ability to empathize. If someone sexually assaulted my sister, I would want to set them on fire.

But I think that's where prison advocacy has a lot to offer. Margot Van Sluytman (2017) problematizes how forgiveness is positioned as a moral good. She argues that those who have experienced harm should be free to be angry, to be resentful, to never forgive if that doesn't feel right for them. I love that approach. I think that prison advocates and abolitionists can and should be here to do the work of reintegrating folks back into our communities. Victims and survivors should not be made responsible for the emotional labour of loving or rehabilitating someone who has harmed them. Communities can and should be able to do the work of supporting someone in becoming accountable so that those who have been harmed can do the work of healing.

There were strong connections between our community work with Word Iz Bond Collective[1] and the work that we both came to do inside prisons. In many ways, performing and writing inside prisons was an extension of the work we did in communities, where we focused on creating participatory spaces to speak about pain and to voice the pain that folks were experiencing in their communities and intimate relationships. Spoken word performance was a ritual practice of speaking the silences, and the communities we performed in/with were deeply impacted by the criminal justice system.

THE POLITICS OF "THREAT"

El: I think for both of us, first of all, we experienced on a personal level this kind of social disgust towards us for being very politically outspoken women in poetry. I know for me, when I first started performing, there were literally all these places I couldn't go because people were just so enraged with what I was saying. And so the places that were making space for me to perform were community spaces with sex workers, or refugees, or the African Nova Scotian community, or all these other so-called marginalized people. And when you're in those spaces it becomes very clear that the same people in those spaces are the same people who are incarcerated and who we'd be seeing in the prison.

And I think on a personal level for me, there was also this connection that I could feel between the ways that my body, which is a very privileged body in many ways, as a university-educated, light-skinned, cis, straight body — but as a Black woman's body I was being policed and repressed because I was perceived as "angry" and "threatening," because you're transgressing both as a raced body and as a gendered body in not performing "femininity" correctly, what Karlene Faith (2011) talks about as "unruly women." And I could connect that to the ways Black women's bodies are persistently criminalized and seen as dangerous. And I would have these experiences where people would meet me and tell me how scared or intimidated they were by me, and it felt very dehumanizing, because it was clear I was just seen as this construct of "angry Black woman." And because I "made white people uncomfortable" as I was once told, it was made clear to me that I therefore deserved any kind of backlash or being banned from spaces or threats of violence.

And my point here is that this is how criminalization works, that some bodies are acceptable, and other bodies — Black bodies, queer bodies, trans bodies, Indigenous bodies, refugee bodies, poor bodies — are pushed out, and constructed as dangerous and in need of control. And the very same forces that criminalize and imprison people through this construct of being a threat are the same ones that also make it acceptable to rape and assault Black women's bodies, because we are seen as aggressive and deserving it. So to me, there's not really this separation between how I've experienced rape culture and how I've experienced criminalization and prison culture.

Ardath: Our notions of "threat" are deeply political and connected to larger systems of violence. Our fear is distributed according to what we are told is dangerous, but we end up fearing what is dangerous to a system of oppression and not fearing the things that are most likely to harm us. We fear strangers on a dark street, even though we are much more likely to be harmed by a partner or someone in our family. Carceral feminism fails us in so many ways. Victoria Law (2014) defines carceral feminism as a movement that seeks to respond to violence against women yet harms the most marginalized women in the process and, in many ways, continues to promote rape culture through a reliance on state structures that promote violence and coercion. Carceral feminist approaches to sexual violence equate prisons with safety. Critiques of rape culture are too often caught up in language that unquestionably adopts the gender binary as the only frame for understanding violence and harm. Man is aggressor; woman is victim. Although it is important to acknowledge and critique the ways in which the gender binary structures our lives and causes harm, carceral feminist approaches ignore the ways in which so many of us are made unsafe and harmed *by* prisons and policing. There is harm at every stage of the criminal justice system, even more so if you are a racialized, queer, trans, or two-spirit person.

For me, carceral feminism is a project of settler colonialism. Because the criminal justice system relies on a binary of victim/offender, it perpetuates Western intellectual traditions that use a moral binary of good/evil. This kind of thinking is the root of patriarchy. It is the root of racism. Western intellectual traditions that rely on neat and tidy moral categories are a form of cultural imperialism. Our fears fall into line with racism. Our fears fall into line with heteronormativity. Our social imaginations can only identify and recognize victims who are white and straight. Racism teaches us to fear Black bodies. To fear masculine bodies. To fear queer bodies. As a queer woman, I have experienced violence in public spaces from same-sex partners. In one case, I remember my girlfriend grabbing my breasts in a bus terminal in front of crowd of people and spitting in my face. I was a ninety-pound teenager. She was older than me and much taller. No one intervened. My girlfriend was not legible as an aggressor. In my twenties I remember wrestling with a male friend of mine outside a bar. We were both laughing, we were the same size, and no one was hurt. I remember three people intervening and stopping him. I remember a crowd of people asking if I was okay. Violence was seen in this case because it fit within the neat and tidy categories we have been taught in a prison society. My cis, white body was protected in this case because the aggressor was masculine. I was legible as a victim. Our failure to understand violence and to heal trauma is the reason that prisons don't keep us safe. If we can't account for all forms of violence, then we can't even begin to think through what kind of interventions might heal us and keep us safe from each other.

Y'ALL *JUST NOTICED* THAT
THE JUSTICE SYSTEM DIDN'T WORK?

El: That's always the challenge of the language of prison abolition for people — because the reaction is often, "So you want rapists and murderers roaming the streets?" And of course, part of that is this socialization you talk about, where we're conditioned by crime shows to imagine that the majority of people in prison are serial killers. But as well, there was a very similar rhetoric at the end of enslavement — Angela Davis (2003) and Michelle Alexander (2010) have talked extensively about this connection of slavery with the prison system — where people can't imagine how Black people will be controlled and disciplined without slavery. So part of talking about prison abolition is also talking about how state violence in general — the police, the foster care system that polices mothers and disproportionately seizes children of Black and Indigenous women, the education system, social systems of surveillance, which Simone Browne (2015) in *Dark Matters*, for example, has talked about — how these ideas of discipline are throughout our institutions, and if we want to abolish prisons we also have to look at how the idea of the prison is so ingrained in us. And ask us to imagine something different.

You made the point about who is legible as an aggressor, and the ways women are constructed within a particular narrative of victimhood. I want to pick up on that with the way Black bodies are viewed and how Blackness exists in an anti-Black state. The title of Ralph Ellison's (1952) *Invisible Man* is based around this paradox that Black bodies are hypervisible because of how Blackness is overdetermined in a white supremacist society, but also invisible. The harm that is done to Black bodies isn't legible. Judith Butler (1993) has this essay on the Rodney King beating where she talks about how white people watching the video literally couldn't see the police beating a Black man — they saw a Black man threatening police. She argues that racism literally structures what the white gaze is capable of seeing.

Ardath: Yes. And so, yes, the prison state is a psychological extension of settler colonialism. It is the logical result of organized white supremacy. The classic argument that I teach in my critical criminology classes is that, in a disciplinary society, the prison organizes power in every possible way. This was Michel Foucault's (1975) argument in *Discipline and Punish*. Angela Davis has made the connection between intimate experiences of violence with state violence, where domestic violence is the logical result of state militarism, and where the exertion of power over others becomes the only response to feelings of insecurity and vulnerability. Movements like Critical Resistance[2] in the U.S. have been really powerful in helping us to think beyond the prison as the only solution to violence and harm. Angela Davis (2003) writes,

> The prison has become a key ingredient to our common sense. It is there, all around us. We do not question whether it should exist. It has become so much a part of our lives that it requires a great feat of the imagination to envision a life beyond the prison. (19)

In this way, I understand skepticism about prison abolition. It's almost impossible to imagine a world beyond the prison state when we have been structured according to its logic since birth. But, at the same time, we must acknowledge that prisons have largely failed at keeping us safe. Incarcerating a single person for sexual assault does not address any of the conditions that socialized them into thinking that it was acceptable to do so. Incarcerating that person does not allow us to resist rape culture because it avoids social responsibility in favour of individual blame. Of course, we know that in rape culture, no one is *born* a rapist. It is something that is taught. Prison abolition, for me, is about focusing on social approaches to untangling how violence is taught and perpetuated. It is about preventing harm and healing trauma in transformative ways so that the cycle of violence doesn't continue. When I think through these things, I think about strip searches and how the bodies of prisoners are often subjected to intrusive body cavity searches. This is rape culture too. High rates of sexual assault in prison should give us pause. We can't make prison jokes like "don't drop the soap" and continue to formulate all of our responses to rape culture on the criminal justice system.

El: And this is one of the ways in which I think some of our conversations about rape culture become limited. We both teach in university, and as women professors in particular, we both end up having students disclose to us, so this isn't to minimize the real trauma students are experiencing. But there's also often a kind of classism and also racism built into these conversations, in that even things like the language of "safe spaces" supposes that Black or Indigenous women are *ever* safe anywhere in society. And part of the rhetoric around the justice system, I think, is that there's an idea that the trauma of going through court or being victimized uniquely exists for rape victims *because* they are imagined to be white, middle-class, educated women who otherwise wouldn't or shouldn't be in court. But that ignores all the ways that Indigenous and Black women or poor women are terrorized and victimized in the courts all the time — how often Indigenous women, for example, are threatened by prosecutors if they won't testify against perceived gangs in their areas, or how Black women will be threatened with having their children taken. So this idea that it's bad when some women are subjected to the brutality of the courts, but when Black mothers have to go watch their children being sentenced, that's normal and natural, that's this huge gap in the rhetoric.

So when people are talking about rape cases as this unique failure of the justice system, I'm like, hold on, y'all *just noticed* that the justice system didn't work? Did you think all those imprisoned Black and Indigenous women were guilty? But there's this idea that going to court isn't traumatic or humiliating for us in all these other circumstances, because the imagined rape victim is still this idealized white woman. And the problem of prosecuting rape is then imagined as this particular way in which that ideal woman is unfairly examined and degraded and how terrible that is for her — which it is — but all the poor women who experience that in court every single day must somehow deserve that treatment. Harm is normalized on the bodies of some women, like addicted women, mentally ill women. And the fact that you have these statistics showing that 80 to 90 percent of women in prison are victims of sexual and physical assault — how do they fit into this narrative of incarceration as a solution to rape?

So the problem is that even when we use terms like "rape" or "rape culture," it's assumed that we're all talking about the same thing. But rape is constructed through a particular lens that has always seen white women's bodies as inviolable, while Black women's bodies invite rape. This goes back to the practice of institutionalized rape of Black women during slavery. So what does it mean to talk about rape in the context of Black women's bodies, where our rape is sanctioned by the state and is built into the very ways our bodies exist in society? Rape culture and white culture are the same thing: You can't separate out the rape of our bodies from the ways Black bodies are viewed and live and breathe in this state. There isn't society and then rape culture, as if those things are separable in the ways white supremacy constructs Black bodies.

HOW WE LOVE PEOPLE IN PRISON

Ardath: I really love Adrienne Marie Brown's (2017) approach to prison abolition as an *outcome* of transformative justice. For me, transformative justice for sexual violence means actually *doing the work* of building worlds where rape culture and prison culture are not our dominant frames of reference for understanding ourselves and each other. The Circles of Support and Accountability (cosa) program here in Canada is an example of this kind of work. cosa brings volunteers together to form circles of friendship and support for convicted sex offenders. The idea here is that intentional and supportive *friendship* is necessary if we want to help people be accountable. cosa calls sex offenders into social space with compassion, and this becomes the space in which accountability is *built* and maintained. What I love about cosa is that they see support as accountability. They don't take up a binary approach of thinking that supporting a rapist means making excuses for them or pretending that they are innocent. The friendship is built on acknowledging the harm that someone has caused. I think this is really powerful. This program was incredibly successful in preventing recidivism for sexual violence, but when Stephen Harper's Conservative government axed the program in 2015, where was the outcry? The only federally funded program that actually rehabilitated sex offenders was shut down, and there was virtually no backlash. This is the trap of carceral feminism. We remain so focused on getting rapists off the streets that we forget that we are raising them in our homes and schools and failing to do the work of unlearning rape culture in our families and communities. Transformative justice work recognizes the harm of violence but does not equate the total value of a person with their actions. It focuses on the behaviour and prioritizes healing.

When I think about the folks who are doing transformative justice work that dismantles rape culture, I think about The Gatehouse in Toronto. The Gatehouse is a survivor-led centre for adult survivors of child sexual abuse. Survivors of child sexual abuse have spoken about how bystander anger in these cases is harmful for the victim. The reality of family violence, and in some sexual assault cases, is that sometimes, victims still *love* the people who have harmed them. So, when we push a carceral agenda and treat the offender as disgusting or disposable, we are also harming the victim who still cares for them, despite the tremendous pain they have experienced. I think that we need to be able to hear these complex and difficult realities. Confronting sexual violence *should* be messy and disorienting, and we need to prioritize understanding lived experiences so that we can better structure our approaches to healing. When we zero in on punishment, we often ignore the acute needs of the victim. Carceral approaches trap us in oppositional optics where we can only see a bad perpetrator and a moral victim and, in doing so, we miss important insights that can help us better understand violence and how we can unlearn it.

El: And there's no place to really be honest about how we love people in prison. I go to court with a lot of people accused of very serious, very harmful crimes, and the court itself is set up in this very binary way, where you spatially are literally choosing sides between the accused and the victim. And I've very much experienced that when you're going in to sit on the side of the accused, there's often this disdain from the Crowns, like because you're sitting on that side it means that you therefore support what they allegedly did or condone it. And you become guilty by association. You really feel this shame that's being directed at you.

And I always think, like, "You have no idea what kind of conversations I've had with this person or how I'm holding them accountable." There's this sense that either there's love or there's accountability. And that you're expected to engage in this very performative public renunciation as the only way to demonstrate your condemnation of the wrong that was done. And I think this approach is actually counterproductive, because people are put in this position of recognizing the complex relationship they have with someone or condemning them. And I think because people can't see a way through this complexity, it feeds into the dynamic where you get people supporting the perpetrator over the victim because there's no way to recognize the love you have and also recognize the violence they engaged in. We're not creating structures that acknowledge that yes, you can love someone who has done terrible things, but that love can also — and necessarily does — include being honest about the harm they've done and the terrible things they're responsible for.

I once had this conversation with someone in prison who told me that his cellmate was convicted of rape, and he confessed that he did it, but he couldn't tell his mom because if she knew he was guilty he thought she'd kill herself. I don't know what it would look like for that mother to actually be able to confront that her son is a rapist.

HONOURING SURVIVORS

Ardath: I feel that. But at the same time, I have supported friends who are pursuing a criminal justice response to their own experiences with sexual violence. I don't think that an abolitionist approach needs to be black and white. In fact, I think that when we take up radical positions that are "morally pure" we are furthering the same kind of binary thinking that got us into the carceral trap in the first place. For me, I think about queering these binaries and try to situate myself in the mess, complexity, and grey area of confronting sexual violence. For some, the criminal justice system may bring comfort. For some, it may bring peace knowing that the person who harmed them is in jail. And, until we have a society that is structured according to a logic *other than* colonial violence, I think that we will continue to seek security from these systems of policing and punishment. However, the system, as it currently stands, fails victims. The emphasis is placed on assigning guilt and blame, and not enough resources are directed at healing for those who have been harmed. Rehabilitation is not sufficiently resourced. The system is cold, bureaucratic, and difficult at every stage of the game. So, when I think about supporting my friends who are survivors of sexual violence, I think about building spaces that are *healing*, and refusing to adopt the logic of the prison. The prison *is* rape culture. It is here that I want to invest: in transformative solutions that teach a different way of organizing our social life and responding to feelings of insecurity and pain. Refusing rape culture means refusing carceral feminism and asking hard questions about what it means to love and care for each other in a world that teaches violence as a coping mechanism for distress.

El: There's also a complete dishonesty, I think, about how we actually treat victims. I think in reality, there's a lot of contempt towards victims, especially if someone refuses to "get over it" in what we think of as an appropriate or timely fashion. In general, there's an initial sympathy, but then there's a sense of "why are you still angry about this?" particularly towards women who are expected to forgive in these very gendered ways. And the prison system actually plays into that because there's this artificial closure where the person is sent to prison, and then you're supposed to move on. People are very uncomfortable with victimhood, particularly in a neoliberal culture, where "being a victim" is conflated in all these other ways with this sense of being a drain on society and refusing to get with the program. Feminists or people who talk about racism are regularly accused of revelling in victimhood. We can't separate that common disdain from how we actually treat people who have been victimized. So the court system actually provides a way of not actually dealing with victims in any real way, because we can push it all onto the courts and prisons, and we don't have to do any communal work.

Ardath: An approach that honours survivors would take the question of crime prevention more seriously. The difficulty we encounter is when carceral feminism presents us with an "us or them" ultimatum that doesn't allow us to *simultaneously* care for offenders and support victims. Increasingly, though, I think that our movements are growing and becoming stronger. I hope that we can hold space for survivors to envision a world beyond rape culture. Supporting offenders with compassion doesn't have to mean that we enable their violence or ignore the harm they have caused. The bottom line is, whatever we feel *has* to be okay. When we acknowledge and attend to how the prison structures all of our feelings of fear, shame, insecurity, and distress, then we can start untangling ourselves from the prison. We can do a better job at keeping each other safe. Accountability can begin when we are honest about how we feel and are honest about our failures.

Chapter 13

CLOSING CHAPTER

Survival and Resurgence

Sherry Pictou

Drawing on the perspectives of eight Mi'kmaw women employed in First Nations organizations within their communities, the opening chapter in this volume examined how Mi'kmaw women's beginnings and processes of renewal stemming from the East are disrupted by colonial patriarchy from the West. In this closing chapter, I continue to weave testimonies from the same eight participants into stories of survival and ongoing resilience. Our survival is represented by the North and our ongoing resilience, produced through a resurgence of nurturing and growth by re/establishing relationships with all of life — our lifeways — including relations with allies, is founded in the South. This is not to detract from how Indigenous women continue to be targeted by settler colonialism in violent ways. Instead, it is to challenge colonial configurations of our existence only as victims by also focusing on our agency to resist and survive — our total existence in a culture that is very much alive. How are we resisting? This closing chapter seeks to highlight what is at the heart of our resistance.

NORTH (SURVIVING THE CONTRADICTIONS)

North is the direction of winter. It is a time of endurance and survival (Battiste 1995: xviii; Hampton 1993). Historically for the Mi'kmaq, winter was when we were very vulnerable and was one of the most difficult seasons to survive; this is the time we would (and continue to) rely on inland sources of food (Prosper, McMillan, Davis, and Moffitt 2011). As Mi'kmaw women our history also raises questions about our ongoing struggles for survival against the painful contradictions of colonial patriarchy explored below (Monture-Angus 1995; Pictou 2017). Is our survival contingent on assimilating to accommodate this imposition or on resisting this imposition? Generations of Indigenous women have struggled and continue to struggle against gender discrimination, violence, and death, and, just as significant, for access to healthy land and water. These struggles for social justice strongly indicate that we have resisted and will continue to resist.

Resurgent Survival

Through our experiences with various processes of oppression, as Mi'kmaw women we recover our hearts — the life soul of our Mi'kmaw consciousness. This journey back to our hearts marks an ongoing contradiction or tension between our life-affirming consciousness as Mi'kmaw women and the ongoing dissolution of our existence by settler-colonial patriarchy.

The earliest contradiction our ancestors experienced with settler patriarchy was between the introduction of a noun-god through institutionalized Catholicism and our consciousness of a living moving universe with which we develop relationships. Our ancestral governance system, referred to as the Mi'kmaq Grand Council, representing seven traditional hunting and fishing districts, reconciled this contradiction by accepting the practice of Catholicism in the Mi'kmaw language. It was not a simple act of religious conversion to belief in a noun-god separate from life forces, because in the Mi'kmaw language, "everything or every person is spoken of in relation with something or someone else" (Sable and Francis 2012: 31–32). This reconciliation continues to guide the essence of our spirituality.

And I had a hard time in believing non-Native spirituality ... but now I can look at both and can respect both.... I realize one thing: I was so lost in two worlds. I felt I never fit anywhere. But one thing I never forget [is] my own learning of my Native language. (Maria)

Finding Our Voice

In relearning how sacred nurturing processes are central to Mi'kmaw knowledge, we learn how the imposition of patriarchal structures in our communities is facilitated by the Indian Act and is at the root of our oppression or lived contradictions between worldviews. For example, contrary to the relationality of Mi'kmaw thought, through the imposition of the Indian Act, the male was viewed as the owner of the house and was deemed to be the head of the family (Voyageur, Calliou, and Brearley 2015). Historically, under the Indian Act, if we wanted to leave an abusive relationship, we had to leave our house and community. It is not surprising then that at the heart of our struggle for adequate housing against these silencing patriarchal parameters we find our voice:

Having to fight for my house [pause]. Four of us living in one bedroom. I hitch-hiked to Shubie, and the Indian agent [appointed to oversee federal policies] — the whole office was full — and I told him, "I want a house!" I was tired of living ... in one bedroom. "I want some answers and I want them now!" ... And I got my house. (Charlotte)

And I made a choice that I walk out of my marriage in order to save my sobriety.... I didn't know how to go to the chief and council or band manager to ask for anything.... They told me that I should go back to my husband because that was where my home was.... I told them then, "I don't think we are going back there." (Maria)

Subsistence and Survival

Through the legislation of the Indian Act, men were assigned leadership powers, the individual material rewards of owning homes, and privileged access to jobs. They were never forced to leave the community (see opening chapter). However, it is important to point out that many of our people — men, women, and their children — continued to migrate with the availability of food and other natural resources for subsistence. Many travelled (and continue to do so) to local urban centres to find work (Guillemin 1975; Satzewich and Wotherspoon 1993).

It was not until the 1960s, when many legal challenges over land commenced, and when the federal government came under pressure by Indigenous organizations protesting and resisting assimilation policies, that social assistance and employment programs were initiated on reserves. Unfortunately, in many cases, these programs reinforced male privilege such as in elected or managerial positions (Monture-Angus 1995; Pictou 1996). Therefore, women found it even more necessary to continue to migrate in attempts to provide for their children and to protect themselves and their children from the impacts of substance abuse and mental, physical, and sexual abuse experienced within these extensions of colonial patriarchy:

> I quit drinking. I kept working. I had a place of my own eventually. I had a nice apartment. I bought my own stuff. Then I worked at [housekeeping] for another year.... I had my mother look after the kids.... I paid my mother to look after the kids ... to buy them stuff and whatever they needed.... I ended up in treatment [for addictions]. (Ann)

> She [mother] helped take care of them [children] while I was always out having these half-assed jobs, and I might make $17.00 in a week and I'd have half for myself and I'd send the rest home to her. (Charlotte)

Many of us continue to take on this role as the main provider for our families in living in or moving back to our communities by finding jobs working in agencies or organizations:

At least half of my cheque goes towards them [parents and sib-
lings]. And that changes me, like I guess people would say ...
"You're not living on your own [because you are single]. You
don't know how to live on your own." But I always think of them
[family].... You can be independent but yet at home. (Beonka)

Recovering Our Roles as Mothers

Through our lived oppression as Mi'kmaw children and later as women,
we have experienced poverty and physical, mental, and sexual abuse,
along with substance abuse directly or with our families. Yet through
these experiences some of us recover our capacity to give life and to carry
out mothering or nurturing processes. In other words, by reflecting on
our own childhood experiences we relearn our responsibility as mothers:

We lived in a car, we lived in an old shack, then we lived in a
tent, then we lived in a barn.... That Christmas we didn't have
anything for the kids. And I will never forget that Christmas....
It was painful because of the fact that we did not have anything
for the kids.... I couldn't even buy my kids gifts because I wasn't
given money. And that was very painful, and I will never forget
it. But it never happened again, and I made sure of it no matter
what. (Ann)

I had to go out and look for food. I went into some stores and
stole food ... literally stole food.... [Later] I took in ... teenagers
... or adults. Took in the teenagers that was having problems with
their families.... Because I would want somebody to do that to
me. (Charlotte)

Recovering Our Sacred Identity with Community

Underscoring colonial patriarchy is an element of dehumanization that
we have experienced within our own communities. Yet the community is
also what lies at the heart of our consciousness, rooted in the sacredness
of living forces that evolve out of giving life, mothering, and nurturing
relationships. Though we continue to experience the intrusion of oppressive colonial patriarchal forces, we still identify with a sense of belonging

in our communities. Many of us who had left the community because of the hardships we faced, or who had been legally forced to leave, returned for economic reasons but also to recover our hearts and provide our children with the opportunity to discover their hearts:

> The reason I moved back on the reserve was to have a place for my kids.... The way I talk to my grandchildren ... to be proud for being an Indian. (Maria)

> I have lived off the reserve.... Instead of the support being there, they wanted to hear the struggles over and over. Like, "How did you survive? I couldn't have never done that." [Yet] I could come into my community and talk to one of my Native people. The support was here and the understanding. (Monica)

> Even all that bad stuff, I would never leave it ... because I was brought up here, this is my family.... No matter what happens, we still stick together.... I want them [children] to be proud of who they are, because I believe the Mi'kmaq is very spiritual. I never want my children to lose that.... Respect Mother Earth, water. Don't take anything for granted. (Mary)

> What made me learn living [in] the community was that my sense of my family and my community were very, very important to me and what made me was community. I felt comfortable with them. I didn't have to prove myself.... I still knew I belonged there.... My roots and everything are in the community. (Beonka)

Decolonizing Education

As Mi'kmaw women, we have suffered racism and ignorance within academic institutions. In 2017, Masuma Khan, non-Indigenous vice-president of the Dalhousie University Student Union, was the target of violent racist statements and threats on social media and potential disciplinary action for supporting Indigenous students' position against celebrating the founding of Canada (Bundale 2017). Yet through these learning experiences of racism and ignorance, we find our voice of resistance. For Beonka, this was speaking out to a professor who, like many others, portrayed all Indigenous communities as victimized and living in abject poverty with poor housing and no running water:

> Even for an educated person, she [professor] was really igno-
> rant.... I've learned that some people ... [have] never really
> been to a Native community and they listen to this woman with
> a PhD and they automatically assume she's right.... If you let
> this continue and if I didn't speak out.... Then she apologized in
> front of the class ... and [said] that she was gonna visit some of
> the communities.

While many Indigenous communities across Canada continue to experience poor living conditions and inadequate access to water, it is not the case for all. These stereotyped generalizations about Indigenous communities obscure their diversity and the diversity of their cultures. Just as significant, the greatest injustice and neglect in addressing missing and murdered Indigenous women is the predominant sexist and racist stereotypes that degrade and devalue, if not blame, Indigenous women for the perpetration of violence against them and their own deaths (The National Inquiry into Missing and Murdered Indigenous Women and Girls 2017).

Politics of Identity

Though strides have been made in increased economic and political participation by Indigenous women, the Indian Act continues to facili-tate several layers of oppression underscored by our ongoing struggle in maintaining our cultural identity against an enforced identity of inferior-ity. For example, we lose entitlement to programs, services, and in some cases employment opportunities by living off reserve, even if we were raised on the reserve. "The on/off reserve distinction is a construction of Canadian law. 'Indians' did not dream up reserves, The Canadian gov-ernment did in an effort to ensure controlled 'settlement' of our lands" (Monture-Angus 1995: 47). Furthermore, it is important to remember that First Nations women, their children, and grandchildren who lost status because of marriage to a non-Indigenous man can file for status based only on lineage traced no further back than 1951 (see opening chapter).

These types of policies further divide our people and fuel conflict in and with our communities.

This multilayered oppression encompasses a tension between our relational worldview and the external policies that dictate our material conditions. Yet, if we did not have the reserves, would our consciousness of moving living forces as reflected in our culture and language have survived? This is a contradiction within a contradiction: the denial of individual property rights (which our ancestors opposed) maintains our relational worldview, which continues to inform our sense of community and belonging. This sense of community, whether on reserve or off, provides us with the strength to resist and survive.

SOUTH (NURTURING, GROWTH, AND REGENERATION)

South is the direction of summer when life is at its fullest. Summer is also when we are able to travel and nurture our relationships — our ways of knowing (Battiste 1995: xvi). Therefore, our survival and our relationships with one another encompass the nurturing of sacred reciprocal relationships with each other and with the land (Pictou 2017).

> When I was only a small child, he [grandfather] would take me for walks near a river where we lived. He talked about Mother Earth.... She will sustain you, she will keep on giving you life as long as you treat her with respect. (Little Bird)

> You don't need all the material things in life, you know, to have a close relationship, to be a happy family. It taught us love is not material things. It's what you have and what you do with it. (Beonka)

We continue to rely on our ability to move and migrate with the cycles of the seasons for subsistence (Pictou 2017). This concept of developing relationships with moving life forces is regarded as sacred or spiritual for many Indigenous Peoples. Western worldviews of ownership are based on "the political [and economic] owner of the land" as opposed to the "spiritual owner of the land" (Deloria 1994: 76). The continuous spiritual nurturing of relationships with the land also encompasses a continuing spiritual nurturing of relationships between genders. These processes evolve out of our consciousness as women and with earth as givers of life, mothering, and nurturing (Moreton-Robinson 2015).

Regenerating Our Roles as Mi'kmaw Women

> You ... who look on me as ... infirm and weak, ... know that in what I am, the Creator has given to my share talents and properties at least as much worth as yours. I have the faculty of bringing into the world warriors, great hunters, and admirable managers of canoes. (Mi'kmaw woman at feast, in Maillard 1758: 15–16)

Traditionally, the Mi'kmaw male role as hunter, warrior, and protector was interdependent on the Mi'kmaw woman's role as giver and nurturer of life within both a human and earth context. But this does not mean that women were not also hunters, warriors, and protectors. While the men were off hunting or at war, the women fed and protected their people. At other times this was a collective effort of both men and women. Based on my recent research, women are increasingly reasserting themselves as food harvesters and ever more so in leading struggles to protect land and water sources of food against development (Pictou 2017).

As sources of food have come under constant threat and been depleted, many of our families have experienced hunger, and thus developed a deep respect for food (see also Pictou 2017):

> I always tell my kids that when we put food out, it is important that it never goes to waste. (Maria)

> Right now? I always made damn sure I got extra on the stove. (Charlotte)

> My father was the last person to eat.... He shared everything. (Little Bird)

Nurturing Children as a Communal Responsibility

Central to mothering processes of women and earth is a nurturing respect in children's ability to learn through observation and experience. In developing relationships with living forces, we learn and relearn how important it is to provide our children with opportunities to observe and experience life:

> They live within the environment and spiritual realms, and are ... to be aware and live in harmony with both nature (including the unconscious, the unknown) and people. They are taught to observe, to look at the trees, rocks, water and sky ... yet most important is not their good environment, but instead their own goodness which contributes to the overall harmony of life. (Henderson, Marshall, and Alford 1993: 51)

Further, we remember how the responsibility for raising children lies with all members of the community. This communal responsibility is a process many of us witnessed as children and cherish in raising our own children:

> It is nice to know that somebody else cares enough for your children ... no harm will come to them. That you don't get that ... in the non-Native community.... We had respect. We were brought up with a lot of respect.... To me, growing up, it was nice. We go over to [Mi'kmaw woman Elder] and watch her make baskets. She would explain and we would watch her.... The discipline.... They would watch us. (Little Bird)

> The only reason I came back ... was for my children.... There were always people, places, homes, neighbours that watched your children. (Ann)

Spiritual Essences of Intergenerational Learning

In many cases, we remember our families and especially our grandmothers and mothers being central to our childhood learning experiences in terms of observing and practising the spiritual essences of love and respect:

On a beautiful night, all the stars, she [mother] would just lie outside and watch the stars as a source of entertainment. And, you know, she would try to find all the constellations. And then she taught us, even with my grandma, like how to predict the weather by just looking at … how the clouds covered the moon. (Beonka)

Today, I realize how much she [grandmother] loved me and the way she was determined to teach me something.… If I did wrong, she wouldn't come out hollering and screaming or take the strap out. She would say … "Come here.… Just sit down beside me. I need to talk to you." And even simple things … I used to call them little things, but today I find they're big and I learned a lot from them. (Mary)

Perhaps one of the most fundamental ways we learned as children was through storytelling, which is something we have learned to value in raising our children and grandchildren:

And I guess something we all do, even today … and like some of the storytelling … she [mother] learned from her grandmother. And some of them [stories] nobody has even heard because [they are not written and] they've been passed down from generations from her family. And even [younger sister] knows them today. (Beonka)

Now you know by your experience that you're telling stories.… You're falling right into the same situation that your elders [did]. (Charlotte)

Paula Gunn Allen (1992) reinterprets Indigenous oral traditions, literature, myths, and legends from a tribal and feminist perspective to establish how the feminine was central in many tribal societies (see also Emberley 1993; Bataille and Sands 1984). Indigenous oral traditions are often discounted in dominant knowledge production practices as fictitious or inferior knowledge, especially if the myth or tradition indicates women are powerful. In Ruth Holmes Whitehead's (1988: 17) *Stories from the Six Worlds: Micmac Legends*, there are countless representations of Mi'kmaw women's sacred roles "through the myth and within the myth" in the creation and development of relationships with life. Allen (1992: 225) describes oral tradition as a "continuous flux, which enables it to accommodate itself to the real circumstances of a people's lives." In this respect, oral traditions represent a continuous sacred movement of living forces throughout time.

Other forms of expressing the sacredness of women-centredness were petroglyphs (rock drawings), decorative clothing, and drawings on our *wikuom* (wigwam), mostly crafted by women. Unfortunately, these expressions do not get noted as being sacred expressions of women in non-Indigenous interpretations. For example, Marion Robertson (1973: Figures 181–184) notes in her *Rock Drawings of the Micmac Indians* that "although there is no reference among the early writers of special ceremonies for women, and women attended neither feasts nor councils, these figures seem to be women participants in a ritual ceremony wearing ceremonial costumes." Many of our dances, ceremonies, and ritual practices that we are regenerating today represent our roles inherent in our scared knowledge of the universe.

Conclusion: Allies in Indigenous Struggles for Dis/Consent

In many cases Mi'kmaw women attribute learning how to heal and recover from intergenerational trauma and experience with addictions to support from Indigenous and non-Indigenous friends, family, and professional counsellors (Pictou 1996). Tuma Young (2016) explains how the practice of building allies stems from our relational worldview. In other words, developing alliances with human and non-human life forces was a necessary strategy for survival (see also Pictou 2017). Indeed, regenerating our relational practice of building allies is apparent in our ongoing struggles against colonial patriarchy, whether it is healing or seeking justice for missing and murdered Indigenous women and two-spirited people or fighting the industrial threats to sources of water and food for all peoples — Indigenous and non-Indigenous. These collaborations are critical in disconsenting with state and industrial corporations or the "judicial-political framework" (Moreton-Robinson 2015: 126).

One of the most problematic issues with state-driven processes — such as treaty and land claim negotiations, and truth and reconciliation policies in response to the tragic intergenerational impacts of residential schools

— is that they greatly risk perpetuating the oppression of Indigenous women. As stated in the opening chapter, there continue to be issues with the missing and murdered Indigenous women inquiry, a limited response to gender discrimination in the Indian Act, and an outright refusal to address discriminatory practices against Indigenous children. Furthermore, treaty and land consultation processes continue to be driven by neoliberal policies underscored by privatization and property ownership (Pictou 2017). Moreton-Robinson (2015: 185) describes this as a state reconfiguration of Indigenous rights and sovereignty (which are prescribed by the Universal Declaration on the Rights of Indigenous Peoples) and of the Indigenous right to prior, free, and informed consent, in particular. According to Moreton-Robinson, this reconfiguration is being rationalized by "possessive logics" (xii) derived from the dominant white patriarchal worldview of property ownership. Jeremy Schmidt (2018: 1) argues that the federal government's creation of First Nations property ownership policies here in Canada produces "private property regimes" resembling municipalities that in fact give "form to a new reiteration of settler-colonialism." I further contend that if the right to free, prior, and informed consent regarding Indigenous rights is continuously being reframed within colonial patriarchal configurations, the building of alliances is even more necessary. Indigenous women have been disconsenting for over five hundred years. By regenerating our roles in systems of subsistence for food, giving life and raising children, connecting with our communities, and building alliances, we are regenerating a relational worldview as a lifeline for survival and resilience in asserting our disconsent with colonial patriarchy.

NOTES

Chapter 2: Opening: Beginnings and Renewal, Oppression and Fragmentation

1. The four directions are capitalized in accordance with Indigenous usage.
2. The anglicized term "Micmac" was still common at the time of the interviews.
3. This is a complicated issue. See Palmater (2011).

Chapter 3: The Bogus BDSM Defence: The Manipulation
of Kink as Consent to Assault

We would like to thank KelleyAnne Malinen and Sherry Pictou for their invaluable feedback and comments on this chapter.

1. Ghomeshi's original post is no longer on Facebook but was reproduced in full in the *Toronto Star*. See Ghomeshi (2014).
2. For an in-depth analysis of this problem within some feminist theorizing of consent, see Moore and Reynolds (2004).
3. This emphasis on clear negotiation dates back to the early decades of formalized BDSM community culture. For instance, the earliest published BDSM manual, Larry Townsend's *The Leatherman's Handbook* (1972/2000: 248–267), contains a twenty-page checklist of potential activities that begins with the instructions "IF UNACCEPTABLE – Cross it out! IF PREFERRED – Check it. IF INTERESTING – Mark it '?' COMMENT FREELY!"
4. According to Henkin and Holiday (1996: 14), "Most SM [sadomasochistic] practices are as safe as any other form of erotic play." For a detailed examination of negotiation and risk in BDSM, see Newmahr (2011).
5. See also the American College of Obstetricians and Gynecologists (2017).
6. The Fifty Shades trilogy by E.L. James has been widely criticized within and outside the BDSM community for its portrayal of a nominally kinky relationship that is essentially abusive. See, for instance, Green (2015).
7. This ambivalent but effectively kink-negative position is in line with LEAF's history of legal advocacy against kink, specifically kinky pornography (see Gotell 1997: 48–106).
8. For a sum-up of the troubling aspects of Ghomeshi's trial, see Fine (2016).

Chapter 5: The Blunt Instrument of the Law: Consent and HIV Non-Disclosure

1. In Canadian criminal law, a sexual assault is committed when sexual touching takes place without consent. Section 265(3)(c) of the Criminal Code provides that "no consent is obtained where the complainant submits or does not resist by reason of ... fraud."
2. *R. v. Petrozzi*, 1987 CanLII 2786 (BC CA).
3. *P.P. v. D.D.*, 2016 O.J. No. 126.
4. *R. v. Schenkels*, 2016 MBQB 44 (CanLII).

Chapter 6: Curated Consultation and the Illusion of Inclusion in York University's Sexual Assault Policymaking Process

1. The PhD student was charged with sexual assault by the Toronto police in 2015. He was convicted of sexual assault in July 2016. The decision was later appealed by the accused, and as of September 2017, the matter is still before the courts awaiting retrial.

Chapter 7: Military Sexual Violence in Canada

I am grateful to Walter Callaghan, John Whelan, and KelleyAnne Malinen for their helpful comments on an earlier draft of this chapter. I also gratefully acknowledge funding from the Canada Research Chair program and the Social Sciences and Humanities Research Council of Canada (Insight Grant) during the writing of this chapter.

1. In the survey, sexual assault included "sexual attacks, unwanted sexual touching, or sexual activity to which the victim is unable to consent, which occurred in the military workplace or involving military members, Department of National Defence employees, or contractors" (Cotter 2016).

Chapter 8: Surviving Woman-to-Woman Sexual Assault

I wish to acknowledge the financial support of the Social Sciences and Humanities Research Council of Canada under Grant 752-2009-1261; Fonds de recherche société et culture under Grant 131821; Sexuality and Gender Diversity: Vulnerability and Resistance Research Team, based at Université du Québec à Montréal; and the Sociology Department of Université Laval.

Chapter 9: Power Struggles over the Sexualities of Individuals with Intellectual Disabilities in Alberta, Canada

1. The term "roommate companion," also known as "supportive roommate," refers to individuals or families renting rooms at their houses to people with ID. Their responsibilities include, for instance, providing companionship and personal care, helping with budgeting, and facilitating everyday household tasks. Roommate companions are often financially compensated through the rent paid by the individual with a disability as well as some government funding based on the level of care. Participants considered roommate companions to be direct care workers.

2. The self-advocacy movement highlights the importance of people with disabilities speaking up for themselves and self-advocating for their rights. For more information about the Canadian self-advocacy movement, see, for example, Hutton, Park, Levine, Johnson, and Bramesfeld (2017).

Chapter 10: Sex Work and the Paradox of Consent

1. In this chapter, I refer to anti-prostitution activists as prohibitionists (not abolitionists) following Robyn Maynard's (2018) compelling arguments that using the anti-slavery term "abolitionism" could be seen as "white-washed anti-slavery" and racist.

Chapter 11: What You Can Do, What You Can't Do and What You're Going to Pay Me to Do

1. What is referred to here as the "foster scoop" is often called the Sixties Scoop. It was a large-scale removal of Indigenous children from their families and communities by the child welfare systems in Canada and the United States. According to *The Canadian Encyclopedia* (2018), "The process began in 1951 when amendments to the *Indian Act* gave the provinces jurisdiction over Indigenous child welfare (Section 88) where none existed federally." Provincial child welfare agencies elected to remove Indigenous children from their homes and place them with other families, most often white and middle-class, rather than providing community resources and supports. Research indicates more than 20,000 First Nations, Métis, and Inuit children were taken. Many sources place the end of the Sixties Scoop somewhere in the 1980s, but Indigenous children in Canada continue to be overrepresented in child welfare systems.
2. See Hanson (n.d.).
3. The Nova Scotia Home for Colored Children was an orphanage that opened in Dartmouth in 1921. Residents "suffered physical, psychological and sexual abuse by staff over a 50-year period, until the 1980s" (Luck 2018). As of the time of writing, the Nova Scotia Home for Colored Children Restorative Inquiry is underway.
4. The phrase "slap me five" as it is used here referred to high fives, which have been culturally associated with people of African descent, as have fist bumps and a variety of "Black handshakes." The phrase "slap me five Indian" had derogatory connotations.
5. See Savage (2015).
6. See Bosquet (2016: n9).
7. According to the Kaufman Report (2002), the Nova Scotia School for Girls was an institution for homeless girls established first by Protestant churches in 1967 and then taken over by the Department of Public Welfare. Girls who were admitted to the school "had been found guilty of an offence under the *Juvenile Delinquents Act* or were committed to the School under the *Child Welfare Act*." In the period following the 1975 hiring of male counsellors, allegations began to emerge of "sexual and physical abuse at the school." Two employees from the Truro School for Girls were convicted of sexually assaulting students in the early 1990s (CBC 2006).

8. Loney (2013).
9. Ada McCallum ran a brothel on Hollis Street, Halifax, from the 1940s to the 1980s. Representations of McCallum are overwhelmingly positive. For example, Historica Canada commissioned a film entitled *Madam Ada: More Class than Flash* (MacDonald, 1998) as part of the series "The Canadians: Biographies of a Nation."
10. For example, Grant (2015).
11. See Fairclough (2014).

Chapter 12: Tender Places: On the Intersection of Anti-Rape Activism and Prison Abolitionism

1. The Word Iz Bond Collective was a group of Black poets and spoken word artists that arose from Black Scotian communities and featured poets from the African diaspora. Word Iz Bond produced one of the longest continuously running spoken word series in Canada and performed together as a collective on national stages and in community venues for more than fifteen years. They were a founding member of the Canadian Festival of Spoken Word and produced the National Festival in 2006 in Halifax. Word Iz Bond was a pioneer in supporting and promoting Black spoken word poetry in Canada and presented the work of hundreds of racialized artists and musicians to regional and national audiences until 2014.
2. Critical Resistance is an American movement against the prison industrial complex. Formed in 1997, it became an important driving force in a growing movement for prison abolition in the United States and beyond. For more information, see <www.criticalresistance.org>.

REFERENCES

Chapter 1: Dis/Consent: An Introduction

Armstrong, Elizabeth A., and Mary Bernstein. 2008. "Culture, Power, and Institutions: A Multi-Institutional Politics Approach to Social Movements. *Sociological Theory,* 26, 1: 74–99.

Blomley, Nicholas. 2003. "Law, Property, and the Geography of Violence: The Frontier, the Survey, and the Grid." *Annals of the Association of American Geographers,* 93, 1: 121–411.

Duru, Jeremy. 2004. "The Central Park Five, The Scottsboro Boys, and the Myth of the Bestial Black Man." *Cardozo Law Review,* March: 1–41.

Fairclough, Norman. 2003. *Analysing Discourse: Textual Analysis for Social Research.* London: Routledge.

Holley, Lynn, and Sue Steiner. 2005. "Safe Space: Student Perspectives on Classroom Environment." *Journal of Social Work Education,* 41,1: 49–64.

Martin, Patricia Y. 2004. "Gender as a Social Institution." *Social Forces,* 82, 4: 1249–1273.

McKenzie-Mohr, Sue. 2004. "Creating Space for Radical Trauma Theory in Generalist Social Work Education." *Journal of Progressive Human Services,* 15, 2: 45–55.

Pitts-Taylor, Victoria. 2015. "A Feminist Carnal Sociology?: Embodiment in Sociology, Feminism, and Naturalized Philosophy." *Qualitative Sociology,* 38, 1: 19–25.

Razack, Sharene. 2000. "Gendered Racial Violence and Spacialized Justice: The Murder of Pamela George." *Canadian Journal of Law and Society,* 15, 2: 91–130.

The Roestone Collective. 2014. "Safe Space: Towards a Reconceptualization." *Antipode,* 46, 5: 1346–1365.

Schneider, Rebecca. 2018. "That the Past May Yet Have Another Future: Gesture in the Time of Hands Up." *Theatre Journal,* 70, 3: 285–306.

Smith, Patricia. 1999. "Social Revolution and the Persistence of Rape." In Keith Burgess-Jackson (ed.). *A Most Detestable Crime: New Philosophical Essays on Rape.* New York: Oxford University Press.

Sojoyner, Damien M. 2017. "Dissonance in Time: (Un)Making and (Re)Mapping of Blackness." In Gaye Theresa Johnson and Alex Lubin (eds.), *Futures of Black Radicalism.* London: Verso.

Wacquant, Loïc. 2015. "For a Sociology of Flesh and Blood." *Qualitative Sociology,* 38, 1: 1–11.

Wilkerson, Abby. 2002. "Disability, Sex Radicalism, and Political Agency." NWSA *Journal*, 14, 3 (Fall).

Chapter 2: Opening: Beginnings and Renewal, Oppression and Fragmentation

Aboriginal Legal Services. 2017. "Lynn Gehl Wins Court Challenge on Unknown / Unstated Paternity for Status Under Indian Act." *The Media Coop.* <http://www.mediacoop. ca/story/lynn-gehl-wins-court-challege-unknownunstated-pate/36507>.

Alfred, Taiaiake, and Jeff Corntassel. 2005. "Being Indigenous: Resurgences Against Contemporary Colonialism." *Government and Opposition*, 40, 4: 597–614. doi:10.1111/j.1477-7053.2005.00166.x.

Allen, Paula G. 1992. *The Sacred Hoop: Recovering the Feminine in American Indian Traditions*. Boston: Beacon Press.

Altamirano-Jimenez, Isabel. 2013. *Indigenous Encounters with Neoliberalism: Place, Women, and the Environment in Canada and Mexico*. Vancouver: University of British Columbia Press.

Anaya, James. 2014. *Report of the Special Rapporteur on the Rights of Indigenous Peoples: The Situation in Canada.* <http://unsr.jamesanaya.org/docs/countries/2014-report-canada-a-hrc-27-52-add-2-en.pdf>.

Barker, Adam J. 2009. "The Contemporary Reality of Canadian Imperialism: Settler Colonialism and the Hybrid Colonial State." *The American Indian Quarterly*, 33, 3: 325–351. doi:10.1353/aiq.0.0054.

Borrows, John. 2013. "Aboriginal and Treaty Rights and Violence against Women." *Osgoode Hall Law Journal* 50.3: 699–736. <http://digitalcommons.osgoode.yorku. ca/ohlj/vol50/iss3/9>.

Deloria, Vine Jr. 1994. *God Is Red: A Native View of Religion*. Golden, CO: Fulcrum Publishing.

Ermine, Willie. 1995. "Aboriginal Epistemology." In Marie Batiste and Jean Barman (eds.), *First Nations Education in Canada: The Circle Unfolds*. Vancouver, University of British Columbia Press.

Galloway, Gloria. 2017. "After 141 Years, Liberals Pledge to Erase Sexism from Indian Act." *Globe and Mail* 7/11/2017. <https://www.theglobeandmail.com/news/politics/ government-removing-historical-sexism-from-indian-act-after-senates-insistence/article36873032/>.

Gies, Heather. 2015. "Facing Violence, Resistance Is Survival for Indigenous Women." *Teleur.* <https://www.telesurtv.net/english/analysis/Facing-Violence-Resistance-Is-Survival-for-Indigenous-Women-20150307-0018.html>.

Hampton, Eber. 1993. "Toward a Redefinition of American Indian/Alaska Native Education." *Canadian Journal of Native Education,* 20, 2: 261–310.

___. 1995. "Towards a Redefinition of Indian Education." In M. Battiste and Jean Barman (eds.), *First Nations Education in Canada: The Circle Unfolds*. Vancouver: University of British Columbia Press.

Hart, Mechthild. 1992. *Working and Educating for Life: Feminist and International Perspectives on Adult Education*. New York: Routledge.

Henderson, James (Sa'ke'j) Youngblood, Murdena Marshall, and D. Alford. 1993.

"Algonquian Spirituality: Balancing the Flux." Unpublished manuscript, Mi'kmaq Resource Centre, Cape Breton University, Sydney, NS.

hooks, bell. 1988. *Talking Back: Thinking Feminist, Thinking Black*. Toronto: Between the Lines.

Hui, Ann. 2017. "Two More Staff Members Leave Missing and Murdered Indigenous Women Inquiry." *Globe and Mail*, 8/11/2017. <www.theglobeandmail. com/news/national/missing-and-murdered-indigenous-women-inquiry-undergoes-another-shakeup/article36522934/>.

Jacobs, Beverley. 2013. "Decolonizing the Violence Against Indigenous Women." *Decolonization: Indigeneity, Education & Society*. <https://decolonization.wordpress. com/2013/02/13/decolonizing-the-violence-against-indigenous-women/>.

Monture-Angus, Patricia. 1995. *Thunder in My Soul: A Mohawk Woman Speaks*. Halifax, NS: Fernwood Publishing.

Palmater, Pam D. 2011. *Beyond Blood: Rethinking Indigenous Identity*. Vancouver: University of British Columbia Press.

Pictou, Sherry. 1996. "The Life Experiences and Personal Transformations of Mi'kmaq Women." Unpublished MA thesis, Dalhousie University.

___. 2017. *Decolonizing Mi'kmaw Memory: L'sitkuk's Learning and Knowledge in Struggle for Food and Lifeways*. Halifax: Dalhousie University.

Royal Commission on Aboriginal Peoples. 1996. *People to People, Nation to Nation: Highlights from the Report of the Royal Commission on Aboriginal Peoples*. Ottawa: Minister of Supply and Services Canada.

Satzewich, Vic, and Terry Wotherspoon. 1993. *First Nations: Race, Class and Gender Relations*. Scarborough, ON: Nelson Canada.

Truth and Reconciliation Commission of Canada. 2015. *Truth and Reconciliation Commission of Canada: Calls to Action*. <http://www.trc.ca/websites/trcinstitution/ File/2015/Findings/Calls_to_Action_English2.pdf>.

Tuck, Eve, and Marcia McKenzie. 2015. *Place in Research: Theory, Methodology, and Methods*. London and New York: Routledge.

Walls, Martha E. 2010. *No Need of a Chief for this Band: The Maritime Mi'kmaq and Federal Electoral Legislation, 1899–1951*. Vancouver: University of British Columbia Press.

Whitehead, Ruth H. 1991. *The Old Man Told Us*. Halifax, NS: Nimbus Publishing.

Wicken, William C. 1994. "Encounters with Tall Sails and Tall Tales: Mi'kmaq Society, 1500–1760." Doctoral thesis: McGill University.

Women's Earth Alliance and Native Youth Sexual Health Network. n.d. "Violence on the Land, Violence on Our Bodies: Building an Indigenous Response to Environmental Violence." <http://landbodydefense.org/>.

Young, Tuma W. 2016. "L'nuwita'simk A Foundational Worldview for a L'nuwey Justice System." *Indigenous Law Journal*, 13, 1: 75–102. <http://jps.library.utoronto.ca/ index.php/ilj/article/view/26700/19755>.

Chapter 3: The Bogus BDSM Defence: The Manipulation of Kink as Consent to Assault

American College of Obstetricians and Gynecologists. 2017. "When Sex Is Painful." <acog.org/~/media/For%20Patients/faq020.pdf>.

APTN. 2017. "Alberta Court Overturns Murder Acquittal in Cindy Gladue Case." June 30. <aptnnews.ca/2017/06/30/alberta-court-overturns-murder-acquittal-in-cindy-gladue-case/>.

Bauer, Robin. 2014. *Queer BDSM Intimacies: Critical Consent and Pushing Boundaries.* New York: Palgrave Macmillan.

Carlson, Kathryn Blaze. 2015. "More than a Tragic Headline: Cindy Gladue Dreamt of a Happy Life." *Globe and Mail*, May 15. <theglobeandmail.com/news/national/the-death-and-life-of-cindy-gladue/article24455472/>.

Department of Justice. 2015. "A Definition of Consent to Sexual Activity." January 7. <justice.gc.ca/eng/cj-jp/victims-victimes/def.html>.

Donovan, Kevin, and Jesse Brown. 2014. "CBC Fires Jian Ghomeshi over Sex Allegations." *Toronto Star*, October 26. <thestar.com/news/canada/2014/10/26/cbc_fires_jian_ghomeshi_over_sex_allegations.html>.

Fine, Sean. 2016. "Ghomeshi Outcome Sparks Heated Debate Over How Justice System Deals with Sexual Assault." *Globe and Mail*, March 24. <https://www.theglobeandmail.com/news/national/complainants-reliability-honesty-formed-crux-of-ghomeshi-case/article29390608/>.

Fontaine, Tim. 2016. "Canada Officially Adopts UN Declaration on Rights of Indigenous Peoples." CBC News, May 10. <cbc.ca/news/indigenous/canada-adopting-implementing-un-rights-declaration-1.3575272>.

Ghomeshi, Jian. 2014. Reproduction of untitled public Facebook post. *Toronto Star*, October 27. <thestar.com/news/gta/2014/10/27/jian_ghomeshis_full_facebook_post_a_campaign_of_false_allegations_at_fault.html>.

Gotell, Lise. 1997. "Shaping Butler: The New Politics of Anti-Pornography." In Brenda Cossman, Shannon Bell, Lise Gotell and Becki L. Ross (eds.), *Bad Attitude/s on Trial: Pornography, Feminism, and the Butler Decision.* Toronto: University of Toronto Press.

Green, Emma. 2015. "Consent Isn't Enough: The Troubling Sex of Fifty Shades." *The Atlantic*, February. <theatlantic.com/entertainment/archive/2015/02/consent-isnt-enough-in-fifty-shades-of-grey/385267/>.

Henkin, William A., Ph.D., and Sybil Holiday, CCSSE. 1996. *Consensual Sadomasochism: How to Talk About It and How to Do It Safely.* Los Angeles: Daedelus Publishing.

Herbenick, D., V. Schick, S.A. Sanders, M. Reece and J.D. Fortenberry. 2015. "Pain Experienced During Vaginal and Anal Intercourse with Other-Sex Partners: Findings from a Nationally Representative Probability Study in the United States." *The Journal of Sexual Medicine,* 12, 4. <ncbi.nlm.nih.gov/pubmed/25648245>.

Hudson, E.K. 2015. "Cindy Gladue Murder Case Revealed Lack of Medical Expertise in 'Fisting' Injuries." *Vice*, April 20. <vice.com/en_ca/article/yvxzpb/cindy-gladues-murder-case-revealed-lack-of-medical-expertise-in-fisting-injuries-323>.

Hunt, Sarah, and Naomi Sayers. 2015. "Cindy Gladue Case Sends a Chilling Message to Indigenous Women." *Globe and Mail*, March 25. <theglobeandmail.com/opinion/cindy-gladue-case-sends-a-chilling-message-to-indigenous-women/article23609986/>.

Kelley, Matt. 1995. "Wounded Knee Murder Mystery Reopens: Native Americans: Death of Activist has Remained Unsolved Since Her Corpse Was Found 19 Years Ago. Some Believe She Was Killed by the FBI. Others Suspect She Was a Government Informant." *Los Angeles Times*, January 15. <http://articles.latimes.

com/1995-01-15/news/mn-20115_1_wounded-knee>.

Khan, Ummni. 2014. *Vicarious Kinks: S/M in the Socio-Legal Imaginary.* Toronto: University of Toronto Press.

Kingston, Anne. 2016. "What Jian Ghomeshi Did: How a Trial that Was Supposed to Flip the Script on Sexual Violence Only Made Things Worse." *Macleans Magazine*, March 30. <macleans.ca/news/canada/what-jian-ghomeshi-did/>.

Kleinplatz, Peggy J. 2006. "Learning from Extraordinary Lovers: Lessons from the Edge." In Peggy J. Kleinplatz and Charles Moser (eds.), *Sadomasochism: Powerful Pleasures.* New York: Harrington Park Press.

Loofbourow, Lili. 2018. "The Female Price of Male Pleasure." *The Week*, January 25. <theweek.com/articles/749978/female-price-male-pleasure>.

Moore, Allison, and Paul Reynolds. 2004. "Feminist Approaches to Sexual Consent: A Critical Assessment." In Mark Cowling and Paul Reynolds (eds.), *Making Sense of Sexual Consent.* Aldershot, UK: Ashgate Publishing.

National Post. 2015. "'This Was Demeaning': Body Part as Evidence in Cindy Gladue Murder Trial Comes Under Fire." March 30. <nationalpost.com/news/canada/this-was-demeaning-body-part-as-evidence-in-cindy-gladue-murder-trial-comes-under-fire>.

Newmahr, Staci. 2011. *Playing on the Edge: Sadomasochism, Risk and Intimacy.* Bloomington and Indianapolis: Indiana University Press.

Queen, Carol. 2004. "The Ins and Outs of Fisting." In Diana Cage (ed.), *The On Our Backs Guide to Lesbian Sex.* Los Angeles: Alyson Books.

R v Barton. 2015. ABQB 159. <canlii.org/en/ab/abqb/doc/2015/2015abqb159/2015 abqb159.html>.

Ridgen, Melissa. 2017. "Cindy Gladue Case Could Be a Game-Changer for Future Sex Crime Victims." APTN, October 19. <aptnnews.ca/2017/10/19/cindy-gladue-case-could-be-game-changer-for-future-sex-crime-victims/>.

Sayers, Naomi. 2013. "Canada's Anti-Prostitution Laws: A Method for Social Control." <kwetoday.com/2013/12/28/canadas-anti-prostitution-laws-a-method-for-social-control/>.

Seguin, Topher. 2017. "Supreme Court of Canada Asked to Let Acquittal Stand in Cindy Gladue Case." *Globe and Mail*, September 27. <theglobeandmail.com/news/national/supreme-court-of-canada-asked-to-let-acquittal-stand-in-cindy-gladue-case/article36417359/>.

Sloane, Sarah. 2012. "Whole Hand Sex: Vaginal Fisting and BDSM." In Tristan Taormino (ed.), *The Ultimate Guide to Kink: BDSM, Role Play and the Erotic Edge.* Berkeley: Cleis Press.

Smith, Andrea. 2005. *Conquest: Sexual Violence and American Indian Genocide.* Durham: Duke University Press.

Tahirali, Jesse. 2015. "Justice for Cindy Gladue: Protesters Rally Across Canada." CTV News, April 2. <ctvnews.ca/canada/justice-for-cindy-gladue-protesters-rally-across-canada-1.2310333>

Townsend, Larry. 2000 [1972]. *The Leatherman's Handbook.* Beverley Hills: L.T. Publications.

Weiss, Margot. 2011. *Techniques of Pleasure: BDSM and the Circuits of Sexuality,* Durham: Duke University Press.

Women's Legal Education and Action Fund and Institute for the Advancement of

Aboriginal Women. 2017. "Reasons for Judgement Reserved." Factum submitted in *R. v Barton*, June 30. <leaf.ca/wp-content/uploads/2017/06/R-v-BARTON-2017-ABCA-216.pdf>.

Zanin, Andrea. 2010. "'Your Cuntry Needs You': The Politics of Early Canadian S/M Dyke Porn, 1993–1996." Major Research Paper, Master of Arts, Graduate Program in Women's Studies, York University, Toronto.

____. 2014. "Poor, Persecuted Pervert?" October 27. <sexgeek.wordpress.com/2014/10/27/poor-persecuted-pervert/>

Chapter 5: The Blunt Instrument of the Law: Consent and HIV Non-Disclosure

Allard, Patricia, Cecile Kazatchkine, and Alison Symington. 2013. "Criminal Prosecutions for HIV Non-Disclosure: Protecting Women from Infection or Threatening Prevention Efforts?" In Jacqueline Gahagan (ed.), *Women and HIV Prevention in Canada, Implications for Research, Policy and Practice.* Toronto: Women's Press.

Canadian HIV/AIDS Legal Network. 2014. "Rethinking HIV Nondisclosure and Sexual Assault Law — Meeting Report, April 24–26, 2014, Toronto, Ontario." <http://www.aidslaw.ca/site/what-does-consent-really-mean-rethinking-hiv-non-disclosure-and-sexual-assault-law/?lang=en>.

Canadian HIV/AIDS Legal Network and Goldelox Productions. 2015. "Consent: HIV Non-Disclosure and Sexual Assault Law." Documentary film. <www.consentfilm.org>.

Cohen, Myron, et al. 2016. "Antiretroviral Therapy for the Prevention of HIV-1 Transmission." *New England Journal of Medicine,* 375 (September).

Elliott, Richard. 1999. *After Cuerrier: Canadian Criminal Law and the Non-Disclosure of HIV Positive Status.* Toronto: Canadian HIV/AIDS Legal Network.

Eshleman, Susan, et al. 2017. "Treatment as Prevention: Characterization of Partner Infections in the HIV Prevention Trials Network 052 Trial." *Journal of Acquired Immune Deficiency Syndromes,* 74, 1 (January).

Hastings, Colin, Cecile Kazatchkine, and Eric Mykhalovskiy. 2016. "HIV Criminalization in Canada: Key Trends and Patterns." *Canadian HIV/AIDS Legal Network.* <http://www.aidslaw.ca/site/hiv-criminalization-in-canada-key-trends-and-patterns/?lang=en>. Heim, Christine, Jeffrey Newport, Stacey Heit, Yolanda P. Graham, Molly Wilcox, Robert Bonsall, Andrew H. Miller, and Charles B. Nemeroff. 2000. "Pituitary-Adrenal and Autonomic Responses to Stress in Women After Sexual and Physical Abuse in Childhood." *JAMA,* 284, 5.

Loutfy, Mona, Mark Tyndall, Jean-Guy Baril, Julio Montaner, Rupert Kaul, and Catherine Hankins. 2014. "Canadian Consensus Statement on HIV and Its Transmission in the Context of Criminal Law." *Can J Infect Dis Med Microbiol,* 25, 3.

Loutfy, Mona, Mark Tyndall, Rupert Kaul, Jean-Guy Baril, Catherine Hankins, Julio Montaner. 2017. "Statement on HIV Criminalization in Canada. Ontario Working Group on Criminal Law and HIV Exposure (CLHE)." <http://clhe.ca/wp-content/uploads/53.hiv-and-the-Criminal-Law-FINAL-EN.pdf>.

Mathen, Carissima, and Michael Plaxton. 2011. "HIV, Consent and Criminal Wrongs." *The Criminal Law Quarterly,* 57, 4.

Maynard, Robyn. 2017. *Policing Black Lives: State Violence in Canada From Slavery to the Present*. Halifax and Winnipeg: Fernwood Publishing.

Miller, James. 2005. "African Immigrant Damnation Syndrome: The Case of Charles Ssenyonga." *Sexuality Research & Social Policy* 2, 2.

Patterson, Sophie, et al. 2015. "The Impact of Criminalization of HIV Non-Disclosure on the Health Care Engagement of Women Living with HIV In Canada: A Comprehensive Review of the Evidence." *Journal of the International AIDS Society*, 18, 1.

Prevention Access Campaign. 2016. "Consensus Statement: Risk of Sexual Transmission of HIV from a Person Living with HIV Who Has an Undetectable Viral Load." <https://www.preventionaccess.org/consensus>.

Public Health Agency of Canada. 2017. "Surveillance of HIV and AIDS." <https://www.canada.ca/en/public-health/services/diseases/hiv-aids/surveillance-hiv-aids.html>.

Supervie, Virginie, Jean-Paul Viard, Dominique Costagliola, and Romulus Breban. 2014. "Heterosexual Risk of HIV Transmission per Sexual Act Under Combined Antiretroviral Therapy: Systematic Review and Bayesian Modeling." *Clinical Infectious Diseases,* 59, 1.

Symington, Alison. 2009. "Criminalization Confusion and Concern: The Decade since the Cuerrier decision." *HIV/AIDS Policy & Law Review*, 14, 1: 5e10.

____. 2012. "HIV Exposure as Assault: Progressive Development or Misplaced Focus?" In E. Sheehy (ed.), *Sexual Assault in Canada: Law, Legal Practice and Women's Activism*. Ottawa: University of Ottawa Press.

UNAIDS. 2014. "Guidance Note: Reduction of HIV-Related Stigma and Discrimination." <http://www.unaids.org/sites/default/files/media_asset/2014 unaidsguidancenote_stigma_en.pdf≥.

Chapter 6: Curated Consultation and the Illusion of Inclusion
in York University's Sexual Assault Policymaking Process

CASSIES. n.d. "York University — This Is My Time." *CASSIES*. <https://cassies.ca/entry/viewcasepast/17485>.

Castle, R. 2016. "YorkU Draft Sexual Violence Policy for Community Review." Letter to York University members, Dec. 2. <http://elink.crm.yorku.ca/m/1/25044496/02-b16337-c23b4d17b07345968a67ba00490ce9cd/5/569/f5025ba1-c96a-4f3a-b669-14748359164b>.

CUPE 3903. 2016. "In the Interest of Transparency: York's Sexual Assault Policy Documents." Nov. 23. <https://3903.cupe.ca/2016/11/23/in-the-interest-of-transparency-yorks-sdexual-assault-policy-documents/>.

Glovasky, A. 2014. "York Invests Millions into 'This Is My Time' Campaign." *The Exalibur,* Sept. 3. <https://excal.on.ca/york-invests-millions-into-this-is-my-time-campaign/>.

Gray, M., and L. Pin. 2017. "'I Would Like It if Some of Our Tuition Went to Providing Pepper Spray for Students': University Branding, Securitization and Campus Sexual Assault at a Canadian University." *Annual Review of Interdisciplinary Justice Research*, 6: 86–110.

Gregory, J. 2012. "University Branding via Securitization." *Canadian Journal of*

Cultural Studies, 28: 65–86.

Hall, R. 2004. "'It Can Happen to You': Rape Prevention in the Age pf Risk Management." *Hypatia,* 19, 3: 1–19.

Laidlaw, K., 2013. "Fortress York." *Toronto Life,* Oct.: 66–74.

Lebane, P., and S. Cherry. 2016. "York University: Rating Report." Dec. 5. DBRS.com.

Legislative Assembly of Ontario. 2016. *Bill 132 Sexual Violence and Harassment Action Plan Act (Supporting Survivors and Challenging Sexual Violence and Harassment.* <http://www.ontla.on.ca/web/bills/bills_detail.do?locale=en&BillID=3535>.

Sexual Assault Awareness, Prevention, and Response Policy Working Group Meeting Notes. 2015. York University, Toronto, Apr. 29. <http://sexual-violence-response.info.yorku.ca/files/2016/12/Working-Group-Meeting-9-April-29-2015-RE.pdf>.

Silence is Violence. 2016. *In Response to York University's Interim Sexual Violence Policy.* <http://www.silenceisviolence.ca/research-reports>.

Trans Feminist Action Caucus. 2016. "TFAC Statement on Our Withdrawal from the Sexual Violence Policy Working Group." Nov. 24. <https://3903.cupe.ca/2016/11/24/tfac-statement-on-our-withdrawal-from-the-sexual-violence-policy-working-group/>.

York University. n.d. "Policy and Procedures Development Process: Sexual Assault, Prevention and Response." <http://safety.yorku.ca/prevention-response-sexual-violence/policy-and-procedures-development-process/>.

____. 2014. "York U's 'This Is My Time' Campaign Wins Silver Award." *Yfile: York University News,* July 21. <http://yfile.news.yorku.ca/2014/07/21/york-us-this-is-my-time-campaign-wins-silver-award/>.

____. 2016. "Sexual Violence Policy Working Group Issues Draft Policy." Dec. 5. <http://yfile.news.yorku.ca/2016/12/05/sexual-violence-policy-working-group-issues-draft-policy/>.

York University Secretariat Policies. 2016. *Policy on Sexual Violence.* Dec. 14. <http://secretariat-policies.info.yorku.ca/policies/sexual-violence-policy-on/>.

Chapter 7: Military Sexual Violence in Canada

Canadian Human Rights Tribunal Decision. 1989. *Brown v. Canadian Armed Forces* (T.D. 3/ 89), Feb. 20.

CBC Radio. 2017. "Canadian Soldier Who Reported Workplace Sexual Misconduct Facing Loss of Military Career." *The Current,* Nov. 15. <http://www.cbc.ca/radio/thecurrent/the-current-for-november-15-2017-1.4401756/wednesday-november-15-2017-full-episode-transcript-1.4403687#segment1>.

Cotter, Adam. 2016. "Sexual Misconduct in the Canadian Armed Forces, 2016." *Statistics Canada,* Nov. 28. <statcan.gc.ca/pub/85-603-x/85-603-x2016001-eng.htm>.

Davis, Karen. 2013. "Negotiating Gender in the Canadian Forces 1970–1999." PhD dissertation, Royal Military College of Canada, Kingston, ON.

Department of National Defence and Canadian Armed Forces. 2016a. "Women in the Canadian Armed Forces: Backgrounder." March 8. <forces.gc.ca/en/news/article.page?doc=women-in-the-canadian-armed-forces/ildcias0>

____. 2016b. "Canadian Armed Forces Progress Report on Addressing Inapporprite Sexual Behaviour." Feb. 1. <http://www.forces.gc.ca/assets/FORCES_Internet/

docs/en/about-report-pubs-op-honour/op-honour-progress-report-29-aug-2016.
pdf>.

____. 2016c. "Canadian Armed Forces Progress Report on Addressing Inapporpriate
Sexual Behaviour." Aug. 30. <forces.gc.ca/en/caf-community-support-services/
sexual-misconduct-progress-report.page>.

Deschamps, Marie. 2015. "External Review into Sexual Misconduct and Sexual
Harassment in the Canadian Armed Forces." March 27. <forces.gc.ca/en/caf-
community-support-services/external-review-sexual-mh-2015/summary.page>.

Duncanson, Claire, and Rachel Woodward. 2016. "Regendering the Military:
Theorizing Women's Military Participation." *Security Dialogue,* 47, 1: 3–21.
doi:10.1177/0967010615614137.

Eichler, Maya. 2014. "Militarized Masculinities in International Relations." *Brown
Journal of World Affairs,* 21, 2 (Fall/Winter): 81–93.

English, Allan. 2016. "Sexual Harassment and Sexual Assault in the Canadian Armed
Forces: Systemic Obstacles to Comprehensive Culture Change." Paper presented
at Inter-University Seminar on Armed Forces and Society Canada, Ottawa,
October 21–23.

Enloe, Cynthia. 2000. *Manoeuvres: The International Politics of Militarizing Women's
Lives.* Berkeley: University of California Press.

Goldstein, Joshua S. 2001. *War and Gender: How Gender Shapes the War System and
Vice Versa.* Cambridge: Cambridge University Press.

Government of Canada. 2017. "The Women in Force Program, a New Canadian
Armed Forces Initiative for Women." News release, May 31.

Hutchings, Aaron. 2014. "Report by *Maclean's* and *L'actualité* on Sexual Assaults in the
Military Sparks an External Review." *Maclean's,* April 30. <http://www.macleans.
ca/news/canada/officials-react-to-disturbing-report-on-military-sex-assaults/>.

Mathers, Jennifer G. 2013. "Women and State Military Forces." In C. Cohn (ed.),
Women and Wars. Cambridge: Polity.

Mercier, Noémi, and Alec Castonguay. 2014. "Our Military's Disgrace." *Maclean's,*
May 16. <macleans.ca/news/canada/our-militarys-disgrace/>.

O'Hara, Jane. 1998a. "Rape in the Military." *Maclean's,* May 25. <macleans.ca/news/
canada/rape-in-the-military/>.

____. 1998b. "Speaking Out on Sexual Assault in the Military." *Maclean's,* June 1.
<macleans.ca/news/canada/speaking-out-on-sexual-assault-in-the-military>.

Reiffenstein, Ann. 2007. "Gender Integration: An Asymmetric Environment." In K.D.
Davis (ed.), *Women and Leadership in the Canadian Armed Forces: Perspectives
and Experiences.* Kingston, ON: Canadian Defence Academy Press.

Whelan, John J. 2016. *Ghosts in the Ranks: Forgotten Voices and Military Mental
Health.* Victoria: Friesen Press.

Whitworth, Sandra. 2004. *Men, Militarism, and UN Peacekeeping: A Gendered
Analysis.* Boulder: Lynne Rienner Pub.

Winslow, Donna, and Jason Dunn. 2002. "Women in the Canadian Forces: Between
Legal and Social Integration." *Current Sociology,* 50, 5: 641–667.

Chapter 8: Surviving Woman-to-Woman Sexual Assault

Butler, Judith. 2004. *Undoing Gender.* New York: Routledge.

Malinen, KelleyAnne. 2012. "Thinking Woman-to-Woman Rape: A Critique of Marcus's 'Theory and Politics of Rape Prevention.'" *Sexuality & Culture*, 17, 2: 360–376.

___. 2014. "'This Was a Sexual Assault': A Social Worlds Analysis of Paradigm Change in the Interpersonal Violence World." *Symbolic Interaction*, 37, 3.

Chapter 9: Power Struggles over the Sexualities of Individuals with Intellectual Disabilities in Alberta, Canada

Esmail, Shaniff, Kim Darry, Ashlea Walter, and Heidi Knupp. 2010. "Attitudes and Perceptions Towards Disability and Sexuality." *Disability and Rehabilitation*, 32, 14: 1148–1155.

Eugenics to Newgenics. 2018. "What Is Newgenics?" <https://eugenicsnewgenics.com/2014/05/14/what-is-newgenics/>.

Finlay, Linda. 2006. "'Rigour,' 'Ethical Integrity' or 'Artistry'? Reflexively Reviewing Criteria for Evaluating Qualitative Research." *British Journal of Occupational Therapy*, 69, 7: 319–326.

Gesser, Marivete, Adriano Henrique Nuernberg, and Maria Juracy Filgueiras Toneli. 2014. "Gender, Sexuality, and Experience of Disability in Women in Southern Brazil." *Annual Review of Critical Psychology*, 11: 417–432.

Gill, Michael Carl. 2015. *Already Doing It: Intellectual Disability and Sexual Agency*. Minneapolis, MN: University of Minnesota Press.

Goble, Colin. 1999. "'Like the Secret Service Isn't It?' People with Learning Difficulties' Perceptions of Staff and Services: Mystification and Disempowerment." *Disability and Society*, 14, 4: 449–461.

Grabois, Ellen. 2001. "Guide to Getting Reproductive Health Care Services for Women with Disabilities Under the Americans With Disabilities Act of 1990." *Sexuality and Disability*, 19, 3: 191–207.

Grekul, Jana, Arvey Krahn, and Dave Odynak. 2004. "Sterilizing the 'Feeble-minded': Eugenics in Alberta, Canada, 1929–1972." *Journal of Historical Sociology*, 17: 358–384.

Hollomotz, Andrea. 2011. *Learning Difficulties and Sexual Vulnerability: A Social Approach*. London: Jessica Kingsley Publishers.

Hollomotz, Andrea, and The Speakup Committee. 2008. "'May We Please Have Sex Tonight?' – People with Learning Difficulties Pursuing Privacy in Residential Group Settings." *British Journal of Learning Disabilities*, 37: 91–97.

Hutton, Sue, Peter Park, Martin Levine, Shay Johnson, and Kosha Bramesfeld. 2017. "Self-Advocacy from the Ashes of the Institution." *Canadian Journal of Disability Studies*, 6, 3.

Ignagni, Esther, and Ann Fudge Schormans. 2016. "Reimagining Parenting Possibilities: Towards Intimate Justice." *Studies in Social Justice*, 10, 2: 238–260.

Koller, Rebecca. 2000. "Sexuality and Adolescents with Autism." *Sexuality and Disability*, 18, 2: 125–135.

Kulick, Don, and Jens Rydström. 2015. *Loneliness and Its Opposite: Sex, Disability, and the Ethics of Engagement*. Durham: Duke University Press.

Lennox, Nicholas, M. Taylor, Therese Rey-Conde, Christopher Bain, D.M. Purdie, and F. Boyle. 2005. "Beating the Barriers: Recruitment of People with Intellectual

Disability to Participate in Research." *Journal of Intellectual Disability Research,* 49, 4: 296–305.

Löfgren-Mårtenson, Lotta. 2004. "'May I?' About Sexuality and Love in the New Generation with Intellectual Disabilities." *Sexuality and Disability,* 22, 3: 197–207.

Malacrida, Claudia. 2008 [2005]. "Discipline and Dehumanization in a Total Institution: Institutional Survivors' Descriptions of Time-Out Rooms." In Claudia Malacrida and Jacqueline Low (eds.), *Sociology of the Body: A Reader.* Toronto: Oxford University Press.

McRuer, Robert. 2015. "Sexuality." In R. Adams, B. Reiss and D. Serlin (eds.), *Keywords for Disability Studies.* New York: New York University Press.

Murphy, Glynis H. 2003. "Capacity to Consent to Sexual Relationships in Adults with Learning Disabilities." *Journal of Family Planning and Reproductive Health Care,* 29: 148–149.

Nind, Melanie. 2008. "Conducting Qualitative Research with People with Learning, Communication, and Other Disabilities: Methodological Challenges." *Economic and Social Research Council National Center for Research Methods.* <http://eprints.ncrm.ac.uk/491/1/MethodsReviewPaperNCRM-012.pdf>.

Sequeira, Heather, and Simon Halstead. 2001. "'Is It Meant to Hurt, Is It?' Management of Violence in Women with Developmental Disabilities." *Violence Against Women,* 7, 4: 462–476.

Wilson, Nathan J., Roger J. Stancliffe, Trevor R. Parmenter, and Russell P. Shuttleworth. 2011. "Gendered Service Delivery: A Masculine and Feminine Perspective on Staff Gender." *Intellectual and Developmental Disabilities,* 49, 5: 341–351.

Chapter 10: Sex Work and the Paradox of Consent

Balfour, Gillian, and Elizabeth Comack (ed.). 2014. *Criminalizing Women: Gender and (In)justice in Neo-Liberal Times,* 2nd edition. Halifax and Winnipeg, Fernwood Publishing.

Barry, Kathleen. 1979. *Female Sexual Slavery.* New York: Avon Books.

____. 1995. *The Prostitution of Sexuality.* New York: NYU Press.

Benoit, Cecilia, S. Mikael Jansson, Michaela Smith, and Jackson Flagg. 2017. "Prostitution Stigma and Its Effect on the Working Conditions, Personal Lives and Health of Sex Workers." *Journal of Sex Research,* 55, 4/5 (May/June): 1–15.

Bindel, Julie. 2017a. *The Pimping of Prostitution: Abolishing the Sex Work Myth.* London: Palgrave MacMillan.

____. 2017b. "Why Prostitution Should Never Be Legalized." *The Guardian,* Oct. 11. <theguardian.com/commentisfree/2017/oct/11/prostitution-legalised-sex-trade-pimps-women>.

Bruckert, Chris, and Colette Parent (eds.). 2018. *Getting Past "The Pimp": Management in the Sex Industry.* Toronto, Buffalo, London: University of Toronto Press.

CATW (Coalition Against Trafficking in Women). 2015. "CATW Responds: Amnesty International Turned Its Back on Women." August 12. <catwinternational.org/Home/Article/624-catw-responds-amnesty-international-turned-its-back-on-women>.

Dewey, Susan, and Tonia St. Germain. 2014. "'It Depends on the Cop': Street-Based Sex Workers' Perspectives on Police Patrol Officers." *Sex Research Social Policy,* 11: 256–270.

Durisin, Elya M., Emily Van der Meulen, and Chris Bruckert. 2018. *Red Light Labour: Sex Work Regulation, Agency and Resistance.* Vancouver: University of British Columbia Press.

Farley, Melissa. 2004. "'Bad for the Body, Bad for the Heart': Prostitution Harms Women Even if Legalized or Decriminalized." *Violence Against Women,* 10, 10: 1087–1125.

Farley, Melissa, and H. Barkan. 1998. "Prostitution, Violence, and Posttraumatic Stress Disorder." *Women and Health,* 27, 3: 37–49.

Huffington Post. 2015. "Columnist Calls Gunpoint Rape of Sex Worker 'Theft of Services.'" Sept. 14. <huffingtonpost.ca/entry/sun-times-mary-mitchell-rape-sex-worker_us_55f6bb73e4b042295e36b959>.

Jeffreys, Sheila. 1997. *The Idea of Prostitution.* Melbourne, Australia: Spinifex Press.

Mac, Juno, and Molly Smith. 2018. *Revolting Prostitutes: The Fight for Sex Worker's Rights.* London and New York: Verso.

Maynard, Robyn. 2017. *Policing Black Lives: State Violence in Canada from Slavery to the Present.* Halifax and Winnipeg: Fernwood Publishing.

___. 2018. "Do Black Sex Workers' Lives Matter? Whitewashed Anti-Slavery, Racial Justice, and Abolition." In Elya M. Durisin, Emily Van der Meulen, and Chris Bruckert (eds.), *Red Light Labour: Sex Work Regulation, Agency and Resistance.* UBC Press.

O'Connor, Monica. 2017. "Choice Agency Consent and Coercion: Complex Issues in the Lives of Prostitution and Trafficked Women." *Women's Studies International Forum,* 62: 8–16.

Odinokova, V., M. Rusakova, L.A. Urada, J.G. Silverman, and A. Raj. 2014. "Police Sexual Coercion and Its Association with Risky Sex Work and Substance Use Behaviors Among Female Sex Workers in St. Petersburg and Orenburg, Russia." *International Journal of Drug Policy,* 25: 96–104.

Orenstein, Peggy. 2016. *Girls and Sex.* New York: HarperCollins.

Pauw, Ilse, and Loren Brener. 2003 "'You Are Just Whores – You Can't Be Raped': Barriers to Safer Sex Practices among Women Street Sex Workers in Cape Town." *Culture, Health and Sexuality,* 5, 6 (Nov–Dec): 465–481.

Ralston, Meredith. 2007. *Hope in Heaven* (AKA *Selling Sex in Heaven*). Documentary film.

___. 2016. *Selling Sex.* Documentary film.

Sullivan, Barbara. 2007. "Rape, Prostitution and Consent." *Australia and New Zealand Journal of Criminology,* 40, 2: 127–142.

Tanenbaum, Leora. 2015. *I Am Not a Slut.* New York: HarperCollins.

Valenti, Jessica. 2009. *The Purity Myth.* Berkeley: Seal Press.

Chapter 11: What You Can Do, What You Can't Do, and What You're Going to Pay Me to Do It

Bosquet, Tim. 2016. "Dead Wrong: A Botched Police Investigation and a Probable Wrongful Conviction Shed Light on the Murders of Dozens of Women in Nova Scotia. Part 2: Trial and Error." *The Halifax Examiner,* Jan. 30. <https://www.halifaxexaminer.ca/featured/dead-wrong-part-2/#Judge and lawyers>.

CBC News. 2006. "Youth Workers Win Compensation Deal." June 6. <https://www.cbc.

ca/news/canada/nova-scotia/youth-workers-win-compensation-deal-1.626626>.

Fairclough, Ian. 2014. "Duane Rhyno, Lawyer Charged with Human Trafficking, Pimping, Released." *Chronical Herald,* Oct. 2. <http://thechronicleherald.ca/novascotia/1240748-duane-rhyno-lawyer-charged-with-human-trafficking-pimping-released>.

Grant, Dorothy. 2015. "Ada McCallum, the People's Madam." *Chronicle Herald,* May 22. <http://thechronicleherald.ca/opinion/1288420-ada-mccallum-the-people%E2%80%99s-madam>.

Hanson, Erin. n.d. "The Residential School System." <http://indigenousfoundations.arts.ubc.ca/the_residential_school_system/>.

Kaufman, Fred. 2002. "Searching for Justice: An Independent Review of Nova Scotia's Response to Reports of Institutional Abuse." Canada: Province of Nova Scotia. Jan. <www.gov.ns.ca/just>.

Loney, Heather. 2013. "Who Is Terri-Jean Bedford, the Dominatrix Fighting Canada's Prostitution Laws>" Global News, December 13 <https://globalnews.ca/news/1043102/who-is-terri-jean-bedford-the-dominatrix-fighting-canadas-prostitution-laws/>.

Luck, Shaina. 2018. "Nova Scotia Home for Colored Children Inquiry to Take Longer than Expected." cbc News, Jan. 12. <https://www.cbc.ca/news/canada/nova-scotia/home-for-colored-children-restorative-justice-inquiry-1.4484519>.

MacDonald, Fred. 1998. *Madam Ada: More Class than Flash.* Canada: Great North Productions.

Savage, Mike. 2015. *International Day to End Violence Against Sex Workers* [proclamation]. Dec. 17. <http://legacycontent.halifax.ca/council/agendasc/documents/151208cai03.pdf>.

Sinclair, Niigaanwewidam James, and Sharon Dainard. 2018. "Sixties Scoop." *The Canadian Encyclopedia*, Historica Canada. March 21. <https://www.thecanadianencyclopedia.ca/en/article/sixties-scoop>.

Chapter 12: Tender Places: On the Intersection of Anti-Rape Activism and Prison Abolitionism

Alexander, Michelle. 2010. *The New Jim Crow: Mass Incarceration in the Age of Colorblindness.* New Press.

Brown, Adrienne Marie. 2017. As cited in Walidah Imarishah et al., "The Fictions and Futures of Transformative Justice." <https://thenewinquiry.com/the-fictions-and-futures-of-transformative-justice/>.

Brown, Simone. 2015. *Dark Matters: On the Surveillance of Blackness.* Duke University Press.

Butler Judith. 1993. "Endangered/Endangering: Schematic Racism and White Paranoia." In R. Gooding-Williams (ed.), *Reading Rodney King/Reading Urban Uprising.* Routledge.

Davis, Angela. 2003. *Are Prisons Obsolete?* Seven Stories Press.

Ellison, Ralph. 1952. *Invisible Man.* Random House.

Faith, Karlene. 2011. *Unruly Women: The Politics of Confinement and Resistance.* Seven Stories Press.

Foucault, Michel. 1975. *Discipline and Punish: The Birth of the Prison.* Vintage Books,

Random House Inc.

Law, Victoria. 2014. "Against Carceral Feminism." *Jacobin Magazine* <https://www.jacobinmag.com/2014/10/against-carceral-feminism/>.

Van Sluytman, Margot. 2017. As cited in "How One Woman Came to Forgive the Man Who Murdered Her Father." *The Current*, CBC News, March 14. <https://www.cbc.ca/radio/thecurrent/the-current-for-march-14-2017-1.4022956/march-14-2017-episode-transcript-1.4024941#segment1>.

Chapter 13: Closing Chapter: Survival and Renewal

Allen, Paula G. 1992. *The Sacred Hoop: Recovering the Feminine in American Indian Traditions*. Boston: Beacon Press.

Bataille, Gretchen M., and Kathleen M. Sands. 1984. *American Indian Women: Telling Their Lives*. University of Nebraska Press.

Battiste, Marie. 1995. "Introduction." In M. Battiste and J. Barman (eds.), *First Nations Education in Canada: The Circle Unfolds*. Vancouver: University of British Columbia Press.

Bundale, Brett. 2017. "Dalhousie Student, Masuma Khan, Investigated for Canada 150." *Canadian Press, Huffington Post*, Oct. 21. <https://www.huffingtonpost.ca/2017/10/21/dalhousie-student-masuma-khan-investigated-for-canada-150-comments_a_23251247/>.

Deloria, Vine Jr. 1994. *God Is Red: A Native View of Religion*. Golden, CO: Fulcrum Publishing.

Emberley, Julia. 1993. *Thresholds of Difference: Feminist Critique, Native Women's Writings, Postcolonial Theory*. Toronto: University of Toronto Press.

Guillemin, Jeanne. 1975. *Urban Renegades: The Cultural Strategy of American Indians*. New York: Columbia University Press.

Hampton, Eber. 1993. "Toward a Redefinition of American Indian/Alaska Native Education." *Canadian Journal of Native Education*, 20, 2: 261–310.

Henderson, James (Sa'ke'j) Youngblood, Murdena Marshall, and D. Alford. 1993. "Algonquian Spirituality: Balancing the Flux." Unpublished manuscript, Mi'kmaq Resource Centre, Cape Breton University, Sydney, Nova Scotia.

Maillard, Pierre Antoine Simon. 1758. *Account of the Customs and Manners of the Mikmakis and Maricheets, Savage Nations, Now Dependent on the Government of Cape Breton*. <https://archive.org/details/cihm_46065>.

Monture-Angus, Patrica. 1995. *Thunder in My Soul: A Mohawk Woman Speaks*. Halifax, NS: Fernwood Publishing.

Moreton-Robinson, Aileen. 2015. *The White Possessive: Property, Power, and Indigenous Sovereignty*. Minneapolis: University of Minnesota Press.

The National Inquiry into Missing and Murdered Indigenous Women and Girls. 2017. *Interim Report*. <http://www.mmiwg-ffada.ca/en/interim-report/>.

Pictou, Sherry. 1996. "The Life Experiences and Personal Transformations of Mi'kmaq Women." Unpublished MA thesis, Dalhousie University.

___. 2017. *Decolonizing Mi'kmaw Memory: L'sitkuk's Learning and Knowledge in Struggle for Food and Lifeways*. Halifax: Dalhousie University.

Prosper, Kerry, L. Jane McMillan, Anthony A. Davis, and Morgon Moffitt. 2011. "Returning to Netukulimk: Mi'kmaq Cultural and Spiritual Connections with

Resource Stewardship and Self-Governance." *International Indigenous Policy Journal*, 2, 4. doi:10.18584/iipj.2011.2.4.7.

Robertson, Marion. 1973. *Rock Drawings of the Micmac Indians*. Halifax: Nova Scotia Museum.

Sable, Trudy, and Bernard Francis. 2012. *The Language of This Land, Mi'kma'ki*. Sydney: University of Cape Breton Press.

Satzewich, Vic, and Terry Wotherspoon. 1993. *First Nations: Race, Class and Gender Relations*. Scarborough, ON: Nelson Canada.

Schmidt, Jeremy J. 2018. "Bureaucratic Territory: First Nations, Private Property, and 'Turn-Key' Colonialism in Canada." *Annals of American Association of Geographers*. <http://www.tandfonline.com/doi/full/10.1080/24694452.2017.1 403878>.

Voyageur, Cora J., Brian Calliou, and Laura Brearley. 2015. *Restorying Indigenous Leadership: Wise Practices in Community Development*. Banff, AB, Banff Centre Press.

Whitehead, Ruth H. 1988. *Stories from the Six Worlds: Micmac Legends*. Halifax, NS: Nimbus Publishing.

Young, Tuma W. 2016. "L'nuwita'simk A Foundational Worldview for a L'nuwey Justice System." *Indigenous Law Journal*, 13, 1: 75–102. <http://jps.library.utoronto.ca/index.php/ilj/article/view/26700/19755>.

INDEX